The T͏ of an Exceptional Leader

Decoding the Leadership Puzzle

Richard S. George

ISBN-13: 978-1973742678

ISBN-10: 1973742675

FOREWORD

I would like to give special thanks to my editor, **Chris Votey**, who helped bring this book across the finishing line with an amazing amount of patience.

In addition, I must thank those that I have worked with, worked for and had the privylege of knowing as colleagues, business partners, clients as well as Leaders and Followers. You have all been a part of the evolution of this book. I have observed, followed, fixated, obsessed and witnessed your brilliance and utilized it to create this text.

I must also thank my wife, Magda and my daughter, Madeline. Every day I experience leadership lessons from both of you as you inspire me to be the father, the husband, and the leader of our family. Thank you for your patience through my mistakes and for your love and generosity for allowing me to make them.

DEDICATION

I first dedicate this book to my wife and daughter for their contributions to who I am as a Leader.

And second to my business partners, Leah, Rebecca, Doug, Jackie, Chad and Mindy. You all have made this a life worth living and have provided so much inspiration to my life.

Table of Contents

PART I – THE PUZZLE: WHAT IS A LEADER?

Decoding the Leadership Puzzle – it sounds ominous, doesn't it? When you consider the thousands of books written about Leadership, the countless hours spent trying to understand how to lead, and that there's no clear consensus about who is the best Leader or why... calling it a puzzle makes perfect sense. Most people have an opinion about Leadership, but it's rare that two people agree on all the points of what makes a Leader great.

Decoding the Leadership Puzzle is more than a cute turn of phrase. Leadership is a puzzle in that it consists of many pieces, of which that must fit together in order for an individual to be successful (as a Leader). However, the individual pieces are the same for each person, but how you put it together will be different from one person to the next. Unfortunately, it's not so easy to just take what one person has done and apply it to yourself, which is often what people do in their attempts to become Leaders.

Certainly, learning what others have done and the attributes they have embraced as Leaders can help us become Leaders, and we shouldn't ignore the efforts of Leaders before us. This book recognizes that every Leader is different, and each Leader needs their own arrangement of the pieces to work for them.

The kicker is, much like putting together a puzzle, that we feel that we have an idea of what it means to be a Leader, of what that should look like. That image, like the box the puzzle comes in, is what we use to put the pieces together. However, no matter how much you force the pieces to fit together, they won't fit if you work from the wrong image.

Having personally read hundreds of books about Leadership, interviewing thousands of people, and using untold hours of observation and experimentation over the last three decades... I've tried to decode that puzzle, to bring a little simplicity to a complex subject and to distill the best principles of Leadership into one easy-to-read book.

In this book, we will discuss some of the core principles that I have discovered in my search for what makes great Leaders, and then we will move to the twelve common characteristics that make up the 12 C's. While there is no set formula, this book is designed to inspire individual thought about what type of Leader you are.

In Part I, we will explore what makes for a great Leader. We will use a broad brush to paint that image, but it should be understood now that when using this book to define yourself as a Leader, you need to adapt it to your needs, you need to use a much smaller brush to paint the picture. When you have a clearer idea of what that picture looks like, only then can you use the individual pieces (found in Part II) to put your puzzle together.

By the end of this book, you will understand what each piece is and have an idea of what sort of Leader you want to be. You will do this by utilizing each piece when arranging them in their proper configuration.

I will point out now, that just because we identify twelve pieces to the puzzle, doesn't mean you will make use of all them or not have characteristics that are unique to you. The primary idea here is to embrace and deploy only what you need.

A LEADER MUST BE INTENTIONAL

Question for you: Have you ever looked at a picture of yourself (alone or in a group) taken years before and been unable to remember the event? You were there – you have evidence of that – and you can remember the picture being taken, but try as you might, you don't recall being there. The reason you don't recall being there, or barely remember it, is because you weren't there... not completely.

It could be that you were distracted by other events going on, worried about people in your life, or even possibly bored. For some reason, you didn't have your heart, your head, and your feet in the same place at the same time. What good is the picture? Seriously, if it records an event that you don't remember, is the picture worthwhile at all?

One of the consistent themes of this book will be that what-ever you do, wherever you are: **be where you are, do what you are doing when you are doing it**. It's a theme commonly used in movies and literature. The Jedi Master Yoda admonishes his young apprentice, chiding him that he is always looking toward the future, but never concentrates on where he is at the moment.

> *There is a saying:*
> *Yesterday is history,*
> *Tomorrow is a mystery,*
> *But today is a gift.*
> *That is why it is called*
> *the present.*
> -Oogway, Kung-Fu Panda (2008)

With yesterday gone and the uncertainty of tomorrow, all we really have is today. We need to live in the moment, yet so often we don't. Well, the day happens anyways. It affects our lives and those around us, whether we expect it to or not, whether we intend it to or not. The day is better served by being in the day, rather than only looking at what was, or will be, as Oogway pointed out to Po.

Another question: Have you looked at another picture and remembered everything about the day – the sights, the sounds, the tastes, the smells, the people you met? Sure, because you were there... completely there... in that day.

The same is true when we talk about Leadership. As we go through *The Twelve C's of An Effective Leader* in *Part II*, one of the most important things to remember is that people will observe you, people will be affected by you, people will evaluate you – whether you intend for them to or not.

So, the question isn't whether or not your Leadership skills – good or bad – will be seen. The question is whether or not it will be what you intend for them to see.

It's unfortunate that many live their lives today believing what comes easy for them comes easy for everyone else. What thoughts they have should be the thoughts others have, and if someone doesn't have their basic thought, then others are simply wrong or ignorant. Many feel that the requirement to explain further is beneath them. Because of this mentality, it leads to miscommunication, and ultimately, bad Leadership.

This is what is known as the Dunning-Kruger effect, the illusion that low-ability people believe themselves superior, while higher-level people believe themselves to be inferior.

As a Leader, you need to recognize that while you have your limits, you also have great capabilities that you must give yourself credit for. Don't presume that your thoughts should be what everyone has, while also properly valuing your ideas as something of merit.

This kind of balance is important as a Leader. This book will talk in great detail what that balance is and how to achieve it. More important, why is it necessary to have that balance. Spoiler: because as a Leader you will be weighed, you will be measured, and you'll be found wanting.

In this context, wanting is another word for "lacking" or "inadequate". What you do as a Leader will be put under a microscope, with those who need to follow waiting for an opportunity for you to fail – to be less than what they need – so they can, in turn, give you less of themselves.

As such, when you are seen, be there to be seen. What they see needs to be Intentional. Be there in the moment, make sure they know what you want, and any action you do cannot be undone.

Be prepared for this to come back again and again in the book, because it is critical.

Be where you are,
when you are there.
Be doing what you are doing,
when you are doing it.
Be Intentional.

THE LAW OF ATTRACTION

When you set out for the stars
and fall, you land on the moon;
If you instead set your sights
for the moon and fail, you fall
back to the Earth.

There is a lot to the philosophical idea of the Law of Attraction. It's a basic concept that your emotions can control reality itself. Whether your emotions are negative or positive, your life will be dictated by your viewpoint, and things will happen in accordance.

In this book, we won't look too deeply into the Law of Attraction, despite having a chapter with that name. Instead, we will focus on the key aspect to Leadership, the aspect that helps those you lead to do their best. As we mentioned in the previous chapter, those you lead seek to find you wanting. If you don't live up to your potential, then your Followers won't live up to theirs.

They say that a team is only as strong as the weakest link. As a Leader, you cannot be the weakest link, and in fact have to be the strongest link. It is your link that is holding the chain together, and if you falter, no matter how many other strong links here may be, the chain will fall apart.

So how do you become that strongest link? That's not so easy to answer, and in truth, the entire book is dedicated towards that. To become the strongest Leader that you can be, you need to read this book. However, the starting point to all of that is simple: Possess the right thinking.

> ### *All that we are is a result of what we have thought.*
> -Buddha

So what is the right thinking? The Law of Attraction.

Let's break this down real simple. If you tell yourself that you can't do it, then you won't do it. If you tell yourself that you can do it, well there's still a chance you won't do it, but you do increase your chances of success.

Now, let's dig deeper into that. If there is one truth to the human potential, is that we want to be proven right. Whatever we think or feel, we want vindication. We want others to acknowledge that our actions or words were correct, and others would be wise to follow our footsteps. This is very powerful.

Our need for that vindication will manifest itself based on our attitude. If we set out with a negative outlook, we will do what we can to make sure it happens, often by not trying. Likewise, if we set out with a positive outlook, we will do what we can to make sure it happens, often by trying our best to do so.

When it comes to a negative outlook, we embrace "Self-Prophecy". When we say we can't do something, we generally do our absolute best to make sure we can't. Now there is a difference between being told to do the impossible, and being told to do something reasonable (even if difficult). I would love a million dollars. Just because I want it, doesn't mean it will happen. However, I want to teach every person I meet.

> ### *If you think you can do a thing or think you can't do a thing, you're right.*
> -Henry Ford

Now of course, teaching is hard... not everyone wants to learn. Some can be quite obstinate when it comes to learning and will resist because they dislike change in their lives. I could just say, "I will only teach those who want to learn." It's easy enough, and I could be satisfied with that result, but would I still be a teacher?

No.

Being a teacher is not just about focusing on those who want to learn and ignore the rest, it is about reaching out to as many people as I can, and finding a way to engage with them, especially those who are resistant to being taught. I may still fail with many of those who refuse to learn, but I know that if I try, I might reach a few who resisted and opened themselves up to what I have to offer.

It's too easy in our lives, especially in the world today, to only focus on the good and to ignore the bad. It's too easy to just give up when any effort is required. And when we avoid any-thing that requires effort, then we will do what we set out to do: fail.

"I can't get that promotion" means I won't work to try to get it. "I won't make my quota" means I will just do the minimum, and not challenge myself. "The boss will never notice me" means that I will just stay in my cubical and avoid my boss at all possible, so they don't notice me.

Now I won't tell you that if you believe, it will happen. Rather: if you believe, you increase your chances of it happening. More than that, most things in life are a numbers game, and the more you try, the greater chance you have to succeed. Don't let failure be a reason to give up. We all fail along the way.

Of the times I've failed in my life, if I let that get me down, I wouldn't be here writing this book or doing a career that makes me extremely happy. In fact, I set out to learn from my mistakes and continued to put a positive outlook on what I wanted in my professional career, and I got it.

The Law of Attraction tells us that if we are negative, then only negative things will happen to us in our lives. If we are positive, then positive things will happen to us, but those positive things may not come right away, but definitely won't come if we just remain negative. In fact, when it comes to the positive, we will often encounter what is called: Margin of Success (MoS).

The unfortunate thing with most people is an all-or-nothing mentality. Either they succeed, or they fail. What they often fail to realize is that just because they didn't get the one thing they set their sights on, doesn't mean they got nothing for their trouble. In fact, they often got something for their effort, even if they can't see it now.

The idea of MoS is that even if we didn't get first place in the contest, we may have gotten second or even third. In the case of trying for a position at a company, your efforts may not have been good enough, but more than likely your bosses might have taken notice of you. This could lead to a future opportunity, and thus, something is gained.

Whatever the mind can conceive, it can achieve.
-W. Clement Stone

So what does this have to do with Leadership? Is it that if we are positive, then we can become a Leader? Is it that if say we will meet a quota, it will happen? Is it that if we focus on the good, then only the good will occur? If that's the case, where do I sign up...

While there is a lot of truth to the above paragraph, that is not the point of this chapter. While your work benefits from a positive attitude, how others work around you is also a reflection of your attitude. You need to be the example; you need to set the standard. If you are negative and don't think that your team can do something, then guess what, they won't do it. More than that, the team will believe it, because you believe it.

Think about yourself as an employee. Think about all the bosses you've had. While I'm sure you've had some bad ones, I'm certain you've had a few good ones. Think about those good bosses, and think about the time they came to you and told you they believed in you, and knew that you could get the job done.

How great did that feel? Did you feel more confident in your ability when your boss supported you? Did you feel more validated? Did you try harder, did you get the job done?

Once again, we as humans seek vindication. So when our Leader comes to tell us they believe in us, and they are positive in their outlook on what we can do, it makes us believe it ourselves. This right here is where the Law of Attraction comes into play with Leadership. If those you lead see you as positive, then they will be positive. If you show them that you believe in their ability, then they will work harder.

I can hear you now: what about the bad employees? There are always going to be bad employees, and how you deal with them will undoubtedly be different than how you deal with all other employees. I mean, what's the alternative... a few bad apples mean we should be negative towards everyone else? While a bad apple ruins the bunch, we shouldn't treat everyone as if they're a bad apple because a few are. And in fact, doing so makes you the worst apple of all.

I would love to say that it is obvious that no one would do this, but then there are bosses out there that do treat everyone like the one bad employee they have, which affects their productivity. Workers do their best to get out of there and do their best to do as little as they can.

> ### *That's my only real motivation is not to be hassled; that, and the fear of losing my job. But you know, Bob, that will only make someone work just hard enough not to get fired.*
> -Peter Gibbons, Office Space (1999)

Office Space is a fictional example, but talk to your fellow workers, and I'm sure you will hear horror stories about some bad bosses, provided you don't have any horror stories yourself.

The point that we make here is that your attitude will be carried by your employees, by your Followers. They are a reflection of you, and if they are hindered in their ability to perform to their best, it helps to take a step back and look at your approach. Are you creating a positive environment?

> *What you radiate outward*
> *in your thoughts, feelings,*
> *mental picture, and words,*
> *you attract in your life.*
> -Catherine Ponder

Many Leaders feel that it is not their responsibility to create a good environment; their role is to give orders, and others are to simply follow. That is a bad attitude to have, and they shouldn't be surprised if they have workers who slack off. While I'm not saying that you should babysit them and make yourself about their emotional well-being, you should as a Leader set the tone.

If you are positive and confident, then that will trickle down to everyone else. If you are negative and doubting, then that will trickle down to everyone else. So ask yourself, which do you want: confident Followers or doubting Followers? Whichever you choose, it is your attitude that will make that happen.

Going over the twelve C's will undoubtedly help you understand the best ways to utilize the Law of Attraction for Leadership, but here are a few quick things you can employ in your workplace, many of which you will see again throughout the twelve C's:

15

- **Leave it at the door.**
  Whatever else is going on in your life, once you walk through the office doors, it is no longer on your mind. This is expected of your Followers, and the best way for them to do that is for their Leader to be the example, not the exception.

- **Show gratitude.**
  Someone does good work, be sure to let them know it. Positive reinforcement is its own reward, but it also helps workers know that they are appreciated, and they know if they do good work, it is recognized. You don't have to praise them every time, but occasionally will be of great benefit to all workers.

- **Be Intentional.**
  Mentioned in the previous chapter, make sure your actions are the ones you intend to make. Don't do things on a whim and don't be reactionary. What do you want your actions to say?

- **Build Rapport.**
  Your Followers are not strangers; they are your family. Learn their names and get to know them, even if just on the surface. Casually walking by with a hello and their name can brighten a Followers' day. Harder to do in a larger company, but not impossible.

- **Build Confidence in Self.**
  If you're confident in your abilities, then it will show. Successful people like to be around other successful people, and if you present yourself as successful, then others will feel successful for just being around you.

- **Set Clear Expectations.**
  You want people to do their jobs. However, the worst thing you can do is presume that everyone knows what they need to be doing, especially when new tasks are given. Always confirm that Followers know what they need to be doing.

As mentioned, this is only a quick list of things you should consider now when it comes to the Law of Attraction. However, Law of Attraction is only one part of being a Leader, and there is much more to cover.

> ***A man is but the product of his thoughts. What he thinks, he becomes.***
> -Gandhi

WHY?

WHY, is the most important question you'll ever encounter as a Leader, as a parent, and even as a student. Everyone who really cares about any subject wants to know why, and as Leaders, we must answer.

The questions our children start asking as they begin to grow and develop their own personalities is why – and when you answer the question, their follow up questions is often... "But why?"

The question of why is at the heart of every religion in the world. More than any other question, what we ask most of our deities is, "Why?" Perhaps more than oppose-able thumbs, the desire and the ability to ask why is what separates man from the lower life forms.

Leaders take the time to answer the question why, because that is the answer which will provide fuel for self-motivation in your Followers. Once they know why, odds are they will figure out a much better how than you ever could have prescribed.

Millions saw the apple
fall, but Newton was on
the one who asked... why?

-Benard Baruch

However, being able to answer the question of why is just as important as the question itself. This doesn't require you to know the answer to every question in the world, as that would be impossible, and not having the immediate answer can be understood, even by your Followers. So when you are faced with a Why that you can't answer, it is best to defer.

Deferring the question is basically a way of saying that you don't know, but has intent or action behind it that shows that you want to find out. You can usually say, "Let me get back to you on that", and be sure to follow up on it. The kicker is, if you keep deferring questions, then your Followers will figure out quickly that they need to take their questions to someone that can give an answer.

When Followers ask
someone else the Why,
rather than you; are
you still their Leader?

As we mentioned in the last chapter, a Leader sets the tone with their words and actions. What does it then say that your words are no longer listened to because people feel that their concerns and questions are best directed elsewhere? It says that you need to fix this situation.

When it comes to the question of why... it starts well before anyone asks the question. It starts when you yourself are learning the information. Many bosses feel, especially with changes from the higher-ups, that one doesn't need to know the why, they simply must know and do.

Common reasons bosses feel that their Followers don't need to know the why tends to be the belief that it is above their pay grade, or said information is of a sensitive nature (ie., contractual obligation), possibly even that their Followers lack the insight or intelligence to process the information.

For those (bad) Leaders, it basically comes down to a simple attitude: the reason of why is not necessary for someone to know. This is a mistake in thinking because those forced to follow need more than just, "Because", as they are the ones required to follow it.

If a Follower doesn't feel that there is a good reason to do something, they may choose to ignore it. Of course, a Follower may be fired as a result of not doing as told, but how many must be fired when the solution can often be as easy as letting them know more about why something must change?

More than avoiding defiant attitudes among Followers, the use of why can inspire innovation. The question of why is a mentality, an attitude. Some may simply accept a premise and think there is no reason to ask why. This is unfortunate because the question of why is so powerful since it can lead to out-of-the-box thinking.

Many bosses are removed from the work that their Followers must do, and they can easily believe that their status makes them more qualified to dictate what their Followers must do, especially if they were promoted from the job their Followers do.

What these bosses fail to realize, is that Followers can often come up with solutions that the boss may not have con- sidered as a result of them being removed from the work itself. Just because you have the ability to answer the why doesn't mean that you have a monopoly on the how.

***There are two great days in
a person's life – the day
they were born and the day
we discovered why.***

-William Barclay

Those who ask why may seem annoying, as everyone else around them seems to fall in line, and it's easy for us to believe they are simply being difficult, but those who ask why are doing you a favor. They are requiring you to be on top of your game, and as a result, enable you to inspire confidence in your Followers. Plus, more often than not, their question of why is shared among your Followers, and they are simply the only ones brave enough to ask.

Furthermore, do you yourself want to be seen as just a cog in the system? While true that we all have a role to play in the corporate machine, and a cog can be vital for the machine to run, a cog can easily be replaced if it is defective. In truth, it's better to be a tool, as a tool can help maintain the machine, help individual components keep doing its task.

Your Followers need to know that you are there for them, and you have their interest at heart. While there are many things you can do to foster this dynamic with your Followers, being able to answer their inquiry is a giant step in the right direction.

Another reason a why might not be answered is, if there's a fear that the answer could upset the Followers. It's one thing to be asked to do something we don't like for the greater good, that's what it means to be an adult and to work. It's another thing if, what is being asked of a Follower, it is entirely unfair, and telling them why they should do it would result in their disregard for the company's needs. At that point, it becomes clear that you not only need to answer that why, but ask the company a few why questions of your own.

The question of why shouldn't be used as a separator from Leaders and Followers. The question of why can be utilized by Leaders to bring their Followers closer. Having that answer can let Followers feel a part of the company, rather than just the workforce that is expendable. No one wants to be looked at as someone that can be easily replaced. And as simple as it sounds, answering the why is one way for Followers to feel needed, even if the answer itself is less than stellar.

As a Leader, some of the smallest actions you can do can have the biggest reactions from your Followers, and being able to answer why is one of those things. In order to properly answer, it is more than just giving an answer. A mistake a lot of bosses make is to answer what they believe is being asked, rather than actually addressing the why. Nothing makes a Follower feel more disrespected than their Leader blowing off their question and giving information they didn't ask for (especially if they already knew it).

Below are some steps to how to properly answer a question of why. I know it seems rather simple to do so, and yet you'd be amazed how often a Leader fails at this task. There is an entire chapter dedicated to communication, which goes into greater detail on this process than what is listed below, so think of this as more of an introduction to the later chapter.

- **Listen**
  As obvious as it sounds, you really need to listen to what is being asked. Remember that the words 'LISTEN' and 'SILENT' have the same letters in them, and provides sage advice that in order to properly listen, one needs to be silent. While you may believe you can listen and talk at the same time, your Followers will feel disrespected. It might seem an odd paradigm, but when your Followers ask a question, it is your turn to be silent and listen to what they say.

- **Understand**
  Followers need assurance that you understand what they are asking. You look like you're listening, but staying silent and hearing them is not the same thing as actually listening to what they said.

  A good idea is to re-ask their question in your own words, then give the Follower a chance to confirm that you understood, or try to explain it again. This way, a Follower can feel that you were actually listening, and it avoids the issue of trying to ask what you think they asked, and causing issues with the relationship dynamic.

- **Respond**
  Now you must answer their question of why. It is always best to direct the question to the Follower asking the question, but also to everyone else who may be there (if this is a group meeting). That can be challenging, as the individual Follower needs to feel they are being taken seriously, while the group feels part of the discussion.

  It's also important to not try to bullshit your way through the response to their question, as your Followers will easily pick up on this. If you don't know, tell them you don't, but also give them some idea of how you will find out.

- **Seek Understanding**
  So, you've listened, you've acknowledged the question, and you've given a response. That might seem to be all that is necessary for addressing a question, especially a why question, but there is one last thing you need before you move onto the next question, under-standing. Just like you need to understand the quest-ion being asked, you need to establish that your Followers understand the answer being given.

Many Leaders work at one speed (their own) and expect others to follow along at that speed, chastising anyone who cannot as being lazy or incompetent. This is a mistake, as a true Leader knows that everyone learns in different ways, and while they can't focus on everyone's individual need, they do need to try to address their answer in a myriad of ways to ensure that everyone can have a grasp of it, at least for now.

Furthermore, if someone still doesn't understand, a Leader can address it with that Follower in a one-on-one meeting, so as not to interfere with the others who may have questions or any further information you need to relay.

As we mentioned in Chapter 1, your actions must be Intentional, and giving an answer must be Intentional. From how you answer the question to assuring that everyone understands, it should always look as if your actions are on purpose.

A question of why is very powerful, and how you address these questions can make or break you as a Leader. When you answer a question – or defer it – it will look to your Followers as intentional, which is good to keep in mind when you answer the why.

No one is dumb who is curious. The people who don't ask questions remain clueless throughout their lives.
-Neil deGrasse Tyson

LEADING AND/OR MANAGING

Your first response to this title may be that we're splitting hairs. Surely leading and managing are the same thing, right? From a certain vantage point, they are, much like a car and a truck are the same thing. Both cars and trucks are automobiles that have four wheels and use an engine powered by petrol, and yet, I'm sure you would understand when I say that they have their differences. Much like the car and truck, Leading and Managing have their differences, and in being a Leader, the differences are noteworthy.

Originally, the title for this chapter was LEADING VS MANAGING, as it was discussing the differences between the two, but as I wrote it, I realized that the chapter had an all or nothing sort of feel to it, either you are one or the other at any given time.

More than that, given this is a book about being a Leader, it was biased in favoring Leading over Managing, which is ultimately a mistake. I have read hundreds of leadership books over the years and many will tell you to ditch managing and be a Leader, which I strongly disagree with this sentiment. The true wisdom is having the insight to discern which skill set to deploy for the circumstance.

The first thing to really understand when dealing with the concepts of Leading and Managing is that both have their places, and both complement each other well. Both require leadership skills that you can learn from this book, but they are still two different concepts, and understanding what they both are can lead you to being a more effective Leader.

More importantly, even if your primary purpose within your organization is to lead, and while you designate others to be managers, there will be instances where you may have to act as manager. Understanding what a Manager is can help you be an effective one.

Managing is about controlling the situation and making sure that the right outcome is achieved in the quickest manner possible. It is using the power of the position or the title to effect change.

For instance, if your 2-year old child is reaching for a hot stove, this isn't a time for leadership, this is time to be a Manager, to grab their hand before they injure themselves. Likewise, if at work your department faces a crisis and the solution to the problem requires to be immediate and flaw-less to avoid dire consequences, then this is the time for the Manager to step in and take control of the situation.

That is what managing is in a nutshell, but this book is dedicated to educating you, so we are going to go into more depth about what managing is, especially in comparison to what leading is. Obviously, this book's focus is on Leadership, and we do discuss in great detail about what it means to be a Leader, especially in this first section when we attempt to describe what the puzzle box image looks like so you know how to use the puzzle pieces in Part II to make yourself a leader.

Understanding the differences between managing and leading will not only make you a great Leader, but likewise a great Manager if the need should arise, or even spot a good Manager if you ever need to hire one to your team.

The last point is important to note as a good Manager is worth their weight in gold. Certain tasks and situations call for a good Manager, whereas a great Leader might fall short. This distinction is paramount in your role as either leader and manager.

> ### *The Manager asks how and when;*
> ### *The Leader asks what and why.*
> -Warren Bennis

There's a time to lead, and a time to manage. As great as being a Manager can be for an organization, a Leader is still needed. In a lot of ways, managing is the easy way out, or dare I say, the cheater's way. Many not so good Leaders are in fact Managers, and use their position to get their way and bypass the role required as Leader, often employed the "Because I said so" rather than addressing the "Why" (as explained in Chapter 3). Actual leadership is an investment, as the rest of this chapter will address the differences.

RESPONSIBILITIES

The work must be done.

Leaders are the ones that often create the work, they are the ones with the vision and direction, seeing the bigger picture and the long-term goals. They are the ones that see the need to change and monitor the growth of the business, trying to keep the company's head above water.

Managers take the work created by Leaders and find the best way to get it done. For Managers, they may only see the work itself, and not necessarily the implications of it. They are not required to have a big picture mentality and must focus on the short-term perspective.

Leaders focus on the WHY, Managers focus on the HOW.

ATTITUDE

It takes a village.

Leaders are more imaginative and focus on ideas. Their concerns tend to be larger and more future-oriented, of where the business is going, and what they need to do to get the business there. Their main focus is to inspire people to their ideas or convince others that their way is the best way to go.

Leaders need to anticipate possible problems and avoid them at all costs. This is often difficult because the world is always changing, and anticipating problems for new innovations is practically impossible.

Managers hold people's careers in their hands, and often those that hire and fire as needed for the completion of the work. They need to find the best people or find ways to utilize individuals they already have. Because of this, they have to be rational and in control, with the ability to solve problems as they happen.

They measure success by how many projects are done or how many metrics they can meet for the whole team. Because of this, they tend to have a narrow focus on how a task must be done, often favoring what is best for most people, rather than what is necessary for the individual. They don't have time for individual needs, they only have time for what is necessary to get the project done.

Leaders focus on the LONG TERM, Managers focus on the SHORT-TERM.

RELATIONSHIP WITH FOLLOWERS

It's lonely at the top.

Leaders need to have more direct relationships with their Followers, as their insights are crucial for Leaders to do their jobs. A Leader wants to know everything they can, as the more information they have, the more informed decision they can make towards their vision. Their direct relationship also enables them to inspire their workers, to see their vision and help them feel a part of it, that their work is for something greater than themselves.

Leaders often work on their own as opposed to with others, or prefer a more intimate group over a larger team. They may utilize Managers as a go-between, so they only have to deal with a few Managers than a large group of people. They may feel disconnected from their Followers, as Leaders feel they must carry the world and have major responsibilities. A great Leader, while having a great burden, still tries to connect to their Followers.

Managers can often seem disconnected from their teams, often being the boss, rather than their Leader. They are often under pressure to meet certain deadlines and push those under them to get them done.

They don't have time with interpersonal relationships, nor can they spend time thinking about the bigger picture, things need to be done right now, and any way to do it, they will. This can often make them seem mean or unfriendly. They don't need to know anything more than their current project, and Followers who have different ideas of doing things may often feel ignored by Managers.

However, because they need to solve immediate problems, they can often resolve conflicts or opposing ideas, especially among their workers. As Leaders are often far removed from their Followers, Managers can act as a go-between from the Followers and Leaders, often being their advocate for when their concerns need to be addressed. They also enjoy working with other people, even if they don't seem like it at times. They are not there to make friends; they are there to see that the work gets done.

As we can see, a great business needs Leaders and Managers. Often the career path for workers is to go from Follower, to Manager, to Leader. In fact, what you do as a Manager can be great preparation to becoming a Leader, though you need to learn a whole new skill set to be an effective Leader. More than likely if you're reading this book, you are a Manager who desires to become a Leader.

> ***Leaders are made, they are not born. They are made by hard effort, which is the price which all of us must pay to achieve any goal that is worthwhile.***
> -Vince Lombardi

In becoming a Leader, look for opportunities to lead. Leadership takes time and is much harder, but it is an investment of time and effort that pays dividends down the road, and continuously.

ATTRIBUTES OF THE BEST & WORST LEADERS

A leader is one who knows the way, goes the way and shows the way.

-John C. Maxwell

Let's take a break.

I want you to put the book down and think about Leaders you have had in your life. These don't need to be people you've worked with, but anywhere in your life. People that have had influence and was required to give direction to others. These can be your bosses, your teachers, people at your church, PTA, or even social groups. So take a moment and think about all these Leaders you've encountered.

Now that you've done that, I want you to take another moment and consider what attributes they had that made them great leaders. Think of single word adjectives that you would use to describe them.

I also want you to think about what traits they had as Leaders that you didn't particularly like. You might have trouble with the last one, especially if you only thought of the Leaders you like... so instead, think about some bad Leaders you've encountered (or throughout history) and pick out which Leadership traits they had that you didn't like.

Take out a sheet of paper and write down these traits, both good and bad. I have done this exercise with thousands of students in live leadership classes and here are some common answers that I have gotten to this same question. Do any of these match the adjectives that you came up with?

Good Leadership Traits

Altruistic	Creative	Imaginative
Caring	Daring	Independent
Cautious	Determined	Intuitive
Charismatic	Direct	Moral
Charitable	Encouraging	Open
Committed	Enthusiastic	Patient
Communicative	Even-Tempered	Respectful
Compassionate	Fair	Responsible
Confident	Friendly	Selfless
Congenial	Frugal	Skillful
Consistent	Helpful	Tenacious
Courageous	Honest	Visionary

Look at your list. Look at the good traits. How many of those would your Followers use to describe you?

Bad Leadership Traits

Aggressive	Hot Tempered	Prideful
Arrogant	Hypocrite	Reckless
Boastful	Inconsiderate	Rude
Callous	Inconsistent	Selfish
Conceited	Inflexible	Shows Favoritism
Cowardly	Keeps Secrets	Snobby
Demanding	Manipulative	Stubborn
Greedy	No Integrity	Unfriendly
Heartless	Pretentious	Visionary

Look at the bad traits, how many those would your Followers use to describe you?

Perhaps that strong Leader that is Charismatic is also Boastful or even Conceited? Perhaps that Visionary Leader is also Reckless or even a bit Snobbish? Maybe that Demanding Leader is also Fair and Consistent?

Sometimes the words that we use mean in essence the same thing but envoke a different emotion, for example: Someone who is confident could easily be described as arrogant. The difference from confidence to arrogance is how you utilize the trait to make people feel. To know how someone feels, you must have the desire to know. To know yourself... to know others... to have the wisdom to care... all necessary to be an effective Leader.

When we begin to build our image of a Leader, we need to understand that sometimes the picture will use some dark colors blended in with the bright colors. It's easy to imagine ourselves as the Leaders we want to be by focusing only on the positive traits, while ignoring the negative traits we possess. Many Leaders believe that others must change to accommodate them, rather than they adjust who they are to better work with their Followers.

Looking at the good and positive traits of yourself, especially in your pursuit as a Leader, is very difficult to accomplish. We are taught from a young age that we should only focus on the good and forget the bad. The bad however won't just go away because we want it to, and will always be there, whether we see it or not.

The most important aspect to being a Leader is how others perceive you to be. While it would be great if our Followers could point this out to us, most will not. This means it is up to us to discover our weakness and the traits that prevent us from properly connecting with our Followers.

Here's a kicker though, that while we should try to overcome our weaknesses and bolster our strengths as we develop as Leaders, sometimes the traits that are perceived as bad are necessary. Technically, having confidence is a form of arrogance, or being encouraging is a method of manipulation. Being determined is basically being stubborn.

It is a matter of point of view. If a Follower likes you, they may choose the positive words, while a follower who doesn't like you may use the negative words. As I mentioned, we must use dark colors to paint a beautiful bright picture, and sometimes the negative traits are necessary to be a great Leader.

The point of all of this is not to just assign the good traits to the Leaders you like and the bad traits to the Leaders you hate. All Leaders have a mixture of good and bad traits, and even you will have a mixture of good and bad traits. Many will be necessary to do your job, while others may be something to overcome in order to be a better Leader overall.

More importantly, the Leaders you have worked with, are people that will influence you when you take on the mantle of being a Leader. It's good to identify the traits you like and those you don't, because you will fall back on the Leaders you've had in the past, and failing to understand the traits they had to be good (or bad) Leaders will make your ascension towards leadership difficult.

I want you to keep the last paragraph in mind as you read the rest of this book. Now I have read hundreds of books on Leadership – they all good in some ways and bad in others – and the one common thing I see in all of them is that how we will be as Leaders has everything to do with who we've observed as Leaders throughout our lives. This observation is not just those we observed at work, but going all the way back to our parents and older siblings.

Very few are born as Leaders, most learn to be Leaders from the influential people in their lives. That, more than anything, is what I want you to keep in mind as you read this book further.

FAILURE IS AN OPTION

If you never know failure, then how can you know success?

Business is built on the idea that failure should never happen. Companies do what they can to avoid it at all costs, and fear the implication of failure. This phobia (Atychiphobia) is so pronounced, that it can often lead to stupid and even illegal behavior, and can cause a company to go down, all because they fear for their reputation and the potential of losing money. Of course, companies were likely to lose money or their reputation anyways, but it likely wouldn't have been as bad if they accepted their failure, rather than try to cover it up. The key thing to remember in dealing with failure, especially as a Leader, is that you must accept failure as an option.

It's a strange concept indeed, that failure is acceptable. Everything we're told about failure is the exact opposite; that we should never try to fail. That is definitely true, we shouldn't try to fail. We should always set out to do our absolute best and raise the bar. Knowing that, it begs the question, why is the chapter called *Failure is an Option*?

Just because we shouldn't try to fail, doesn't mean that we shouldn't ever expect to. No one is perfect and no one can properly predict the future, meaning that failure is inevitable. Especially when attempting to innovate or expand in new territories, as this requires learning through trial and error, though few companies are willing to admit that. There is always this need that any decision made is one made on purpose, until that decision turns out to be the wrong one, and then there is this need to find someone to blame.

With failure, comes the opportunity to learn. If we can learn, we can evolve. The problem is, we live in a culture that wants to do well at all costs. Because of this cultural need, we fear failure. This is especially true for Leaders, who fear failure, as it can mean the loss of power, influence, or even their career. This fear of failure drives a lot of decisions, which can lead to outcomes that are worse than the failure they attempt to avoid.

The fear of failure is very powerful, and Leaders who attempt to avoid failure at all costs will focus on how things were done in the past. The way things have been done have been proven to work, so why change what isn't broken? The answer becomes simple: the world is constantly changing, and if you don't change with the world, you soon become a relic.

> *You have to be optimistic to be a Leader. You have to sometimes walk into a room with the feeling you can overcome whatever obstacle is there, even if you don't have the answer right now.*
> -Franklin Chang Diaz

This is not to say that failure should be ignored, or even marginalized. Failure is very serious, and should be treated as such, but not to the point that it is seen as the end of the world. Failure requires responsibility, and as the Leader, the first responsibility falls on you. It might have been someone else who is responsible, but as a Leader, you are responsible for all your Followers.

Acceptance of failure is not a means of excusing bad performance or overlooking results that are preventable. If someone has dropped the ball and is directly responsible for the failure, they too share the burden of that failure along with their Leader. As such, the Leader is required to properly address that responsibility of their Followers for that failure, but that additionally requires an understanding of how that failure could manifest.

Many Leaders believe that always having success is how one is defined as a Leader, but the true measure of a Leader is how they handle failure when it comes. This is something we tell to all people, about getting back on that horse, and yet, this is missing from a lot of instruction on how to be a good Leader.

The big issue with failure is how others handle it. How you handle it is very important, but there are outside influences that are looking over your shoulder, primarily those that are above you. You likely have your own bosses to impress, and they have their own bosses, and when failure happens, the response generally starts at the top and works its way down, and like a snowball; the response to failure grows exponentially as it goes down the corporate ladder... and no one wants to be in the path of the snowball when it comes to a crashing halt.

Because of this pressure, many Leaders, especially in the middle of the corporate structure, will search for someone to blame, and sell out their Followers very easily. This might save you from looking bad in the eyes of those above you, but won't save you from the judgment of your Followers. Sure, your Followers can't fire you, but they can make you look bad by not being their best. So what are you supposed to do? It definitely seems like a "Damned if you do, damned if you don't" scenario.

He that is good for
making excuses is
seldom good for
anything else.
-Benjamin Franklin

While there is not a simple solution to this, as all failure and work environments are different, there are ways you can handle failure when it comes that may well appease your bosses, while not selling out your Followers. The below list are things you can do when faced with a failure, whether it is yours or someone else's:

Remain Positive. The worst thing you can do is react negatively to a failure. Failure is a tool, and when you treat it like that, it becomes a resource. Many will be looking to you, whether it is your bosses or your Followers, and how you handle it will set the tone for how others react to it. If you want everyone else to continue doing their job and not focus on the specific failure, then how you act towards it becomes paramount.

Set Your Ego Aside. While it is important to take responsibility for the failure, even if not directly your fault, this is not a time to take it personally. Very rarely is having an ego a good thing, but in dealing with failure, it is always a bad thing to have. This can be seen as trying to downplay the failure to believing only you can resolve it.

Avoid Scapegoats. As humans, we are quick to easily overlook failures that we may have caused, and instead try to find others at fault. This is called Self-Serving Bias, that we as individuals are never at fault, and there is always extenuating circumstances as to why others may think we are.

Businesses can be like this as well, and instead of facing the idea that a failure is a reflection on how they operate, they instead look for someone to blame and discipline that individual (which may result in termination). Thus doing so, the problem ceases to exist.

This doesn't solve anything. It allows a business to continue to allow for mistakes and failures to occur. As a Leader, you need to identify not only who is responsible, but how it could affect the whole business. More often than not, it's not the failing of one person, but the failure of many. You can't fire them all without hurting the company, so how about instead finding ways to the avoid failures for the future?

Identify the Problem. This is the first step towards a solution. Trying to find a scapegoat, it's easy to overlook what the actual problem is. As a result, the failure may happen again. In order to prevent recurrence, a Leader must investigate what happened and answer the question: Why? Once that can be determined, then the path to the solution should fall in place.

Empower Followers. Empower the Followers by allowing them to help in identifying the failure and their approach to the solution. Being on the frontline of the business, as many Followers are, they likely have insight that Leaders may not consider. They may not have the answer (though anything is possible), but if they feel they can contribute, they will have respect for the company and its Leaders.

Identify the Solution. A great way to look at failure is **that it is a precursor to success**. Once you can identify the problem, the next step is to identify the solution. Unfortunately, the solution often requires change, and many businesses are slow to do so.

Many bosses are more Managers, as they think in the short-term, rather than the long-term as Leaders do. While you do need to identify the solution, you may need to come up with alternate solutions that will appease those above you who are not so quick to change. Fortunately, a series of short-term solutions can lead to a long term resolution.

Plan the Next Step. Whatever ends up being done for fixing the failure that occurred, you now must plan the next step. As it is written, the journey of a thousand miles begins with a single step. This, however, can be quite overwhelming, as you may attempt to try to have everything fixed within a single step, and you should try to avoid that. If a failure could be fixed with a simple solution, then a failure would not have occurred to begin with. Instead, just plan what needs to happen next that ultimately leads to the solution.

Move On. The failure happened, and you need to do what you can to address it, find a solution, implement a plan, avoid this failure in the future, but at the end of it, you need to put it behind you. Like any tool, there is a time to use it, and a time to put it down. Failure is a tool, and when the need comes to pick up that tool again, you know where to find it, but just like you don't walk around holding a screwdriver all day in the office, neither should you carry your failures around.

Prepare for Future Failure. It is difficult to know how failure may come about. It's not like we set out to fail. However, we know it'll come, especially in this ever-changing world. The only advantage we have is to prepare for when it happens. Doing so may actually help you avoid failure, by identifying how things could fail when you set out a plan to do something. If you know how it could fail, and it happens, then you can plan for what you do when it occurs.

Murphy's Law teaches that if you plan for five possible things to go wrong, then a sixth thing will happen that you didn't account for, which often seems obvious in hindsight. You can't prepare for everything, but you can try, and you should try.

The big take away is that failure happens. Anyone throughout history that tried to do anything worthwhile, failed at some point. What made these people important, is that they continued to try in spite of the failure. Failure was a way to learn, to advance them to where they needed to be when they finally succeeded.

Success consists of going from failure to failure without loss of enthusiasm.
-Winston Churchill

As a Leader, while the pressure may be on you to always succeed, you need to make the best use of failure. Failure is an invaluable resource. What you do with it will define you as a Leader. However, you will have those above you who treats failure like the plague and rather someone be the "plague bringer" and dispose of that person, in order to feel as if the plague is gone.

The only silver-lining that can be offered by a company that seeks a scapegoat for their failures is that it may be a company on its way to cascading failure. It may be an indication that you need to develop an exit strategy, provided you are not the scapegoat they are looking for.

I'm not saying you should quit, but realize that any Leader that need someone to blame for failures, rather than taking a share of the responsibility for them, is a good indicator of weak Leadership. Do with that as you will, but they, like you, have a responsibility to their Followers, and there are consequences in shrieking from said obligation.

Besides, if you do go for an interview, you know the hiring manager will ask about failures in your career, and how you handled them... wouldn't it be great to give a really great and truthful answer?

YOUR LEADERSHIP BRAND

Leaders are known for the difference or contribution they make in the world.

We live in a world of brands. Practically every object you encounter in your day-to-day life is a brand of some sort. Some are more obvious than others, from the drink you buy from the vending machine to the condiment you pull from your refrigerator. Our world is filled with them, all in a means to remind you who they are so you are more inclined to buy their product again.

This is not exactly news to us, we know this happens, and this has been going on for well over a hundred years. Corporations spend hundreds of thousands to millions of dollars just to get a product in your eyesight just so you might buy it. Large corporations are best thought of for engaging in this practice, but even smaller corporations partake in branding their products, albeit with a smaller budget.

Don't get me wrong, there is nothing wrong with doing this. It's something that works. That brand mechanism can be anything from an image, to a physical product, to an idea, or even a jingle. More than likely it is a combination of many things for you to remember it. Memory is the key here, and because corporations want to be remembered, a lot of thought is put into what a corporation will be known for.

Let's play a game. I'll list some slogans, and you tell me the brand:
- Be All You Can Be
- Can You Hear Me Now?
- Don't Leave Home Without It
- Good To The Last Drop
- Have It Your Way
- What Happens Here, Stays Here

I could have chosen some more recognized ones, but I picked these on purpose (as the first chapter says, Be Intentional). We have in order: US Army, Verizon, American Express, Maxwell House, Burger King, and Las Vegas. From an organization to physical products, to an entire city. Anyone or anything can have be a brand, with the simple purpose to manipulate what people think about anything.

I'm sure by now you have two thoughts.
- First: Well duh! Tell me something I don't know.
- Second: What does this have to do with Leadership?

Put simply: you as a Leader are a product. You are known for what people feel when they think of you. These thoughts can be simple or complex, but they will be your brand. Surely, you have worked with someone in the past who was constantly late for work. Chances are you rarely thought of that person without thinking of their tardiness.

If Johnny always got his work in on time, you knew that this was something you could rely on when it came to Johnny. This is part of his brand. If Beth's work always had spelling errors, this was how she was known. This is part of her brand. You might have already noticed that in some cases the traits of a person's brand were intentional, but in others, it was not; that's a key piece of understanding brands.

Your brand is how you are known, whether you intend it or not.

From here, the name of the game is to **Manage Your Brand.** We draw inspiration from the first chapter: *A Leader Must Be Intentional*, in that when it comes to our brand as a Leader, how you are perceived must be how you intend to be perceived.

If there is a major theme throughout this book, it is that being a good Leader is not easy. Unfortunately, you'll likely not have the luxury of a giant public relations firm to manage your Leadership brand... this, in turn, means: managing your brand is up to you.

How do you make your Leadership brand? As it already has been suggested, your brand is created through your actions. Many believe that success is the best method to make your Leadership brand, and while that can help, if you only focus on being successful, you will no doubt inherit other qualities that will actually define your brand.

Looking over the aspects of failure, we know that if you only focus on the success of your project and do your best to avoid failure (rather than embrace), you will no doubt be known for the Bad Attributes discussed earlier.

When it comes to your brand as a Leader, it cannot solely be on winning your assignments, it is about *Attractions*, about *Answering the Why*, about *Being a Leader rather than a Manager*, about maintaining the *Best Attributes* and over-coming the Bad, and being able to *Embrace Failure as a Tool for Success*. Doing all of these will make for a great Leadership brand.

49

Be aware though, that all your actions are under a microscope. Any failings you have as a Leader will be known by your bosses and your Followers, and if these failings remain consistent, they will be attributed to your Leadership brand.

> *Leaders brands are often the result of and determined by the contribution and difference they make repeatedly during their careers.*

Note that branding is independent of intent – unless you manage your brand by ensuring that what you are known for is what you want to be known for. The Army spent many years branding itself as a road to maximizing individual potential, by saying every day: Be All That You Can Be. Whether they delivered on that promise depended on the individual and other factors, but the Army managed its brand – and you have to manage yours.

Look back at the attributes that you wrote on your pieces of paper for the best and worst Leaders. How much of the branding was intentional? How much was accidental? Most of the time we will find that the intentional factors tend toward positive and the unintentional factors tend toward negative.

Be Intentional!
Be Present!

Very soon this book will be examining the 12 C's of Effective Leadership. As mentioned, this book intersects all parts together, and that becomes important in Part II of this book. When you go through the 12 C's, consider how you can apply them to your brand.

Before we head into Part II, it is best to end this chapter with a few key questions:

What is your current Leadership brand?
What are the things that you do to support this?
What part of your reputation precedes you?
Are you happy with this reputation?

These are all very important questions to ask yourself, but more important to be honest with yourself when answering these. It's too easy for us to lie to ourselves when it comes to describing our true selves. If you wish to be a great Leader, you must start with honesty.

This last question is perhaps the most vital of the questions. Reputation is a tricky thing... it is also a fragile thing.

A reputation that took decades to build can be threatened by a single event.
-John Maxwell

This is the bad news.

The very good news is: if you are not happy with your reputetion and your current brand, you can change it. All it requires is changing the behavior that created it. Anything that has been done can be undone through dedication, effort, and persistence.

*Nobody can go back and
start a new beginning, but
anyone can start today and
make a new ending.*

-Maria Robinson

WHAT ABOUT LOYALTY?

Followers.

No matter how you look at being a Leader, this is one ultimate truth: You cannot be a Leader unless you have Followers. An essential element to having Followers is obtaining their loyalty, which is not guaranteed and is not unshakenable. Many who obtain a position of authority presume that loyalty is automatic, that their position awards a certain level of respect. As we know, loyalty and respect are earned.

Once upon a time, let's say a generation or so ago, when it was normal for a person to take a job when they were young and work for their company for 25-30-40 years. They would work until their retirement. They were loyal to the company, even when the company was not loyal to their workers. The company gave you a job, and your allegiance was automatically given to them for that reason alone. For the time, this was an acceptable approach to life, to be a Follower in a business.

This is no longer the norm. The employee no longer considers themselves secondary to the organization, and Followers of Leaders share that new-found freedom.

Increasingly, Followers think of themselves as free agents, not as dependent underlings, and they act accordingly...
-Barbara Kellerman, Harvard University

53

The individual today perceives themselves as equals to the company, and Followers are equal to their Leaders. This means that maintaining loyalty is far more difficult. It is never a given, and it requires constant effort.

Now, we could discuss the complex socio-political trends which have served to bring about this change of an individual once being bound to the company to the individual now believing to be equal to their company, some of which could be describe as inevitable based on the increase of life expectancy or even overall quality of life. Other reasons that can be discussed is economic realities and natural changes in society, some of which are the result of political and social actions taken over the course of the last 50 years. Sociologists and political scientists debate the reasons why, but for the purposes of this book, the why, ironically, is not important.

Why loyalty is more difficult to obtain is not the issue you should focus on; rather, a Leader needs to focus on what loyalty is today and how to obtain it, which will make you a more effective Leader. Now could you study history and political science in reference to this evolution of loyalty amongst Followers and gain a greater understanding? Absolutely. Is it a requirement for you to study this in order to be a great Leader? No, not at all.

So the most important question we can ask in this chapter: How do you, as the Leader, earn the loyalty of your Followers? In order to gain loyalty, we need to understand what loyalty is, or rather, learn about disloyalty. This is important, as many would-be Leaders believe that their Followers disrespect them, and thus are disloyal, for doing things that a Follower should be doing, or need to do to be more productive. Behaviors that Leaders should be encouraging are thus seen as being disloyal and Followers are likely punished, which turns into disloyalty by other Followers.

The following are things that might seem disloyal from Followers:
- Refusing to Follow an Order
- Questioning What a Leader is Saying
- Having a Difference of Opinion
- Talking About the Boss Behind Their Back

These things can easily seem as if the Follower lacks loyalty to you as the Leader if they do any of the following, but it is best to remember that your Followers are human and not mindless androids that do everything you say. One day we might have robotic workers, but today is not the day. Though I don't know about you, but I'm not too interested in a Follower that doesn't have a mind for themselves.

Refusing to Follow an Order, can be seen as disloyalty, but the question becomes, is the Follower in their right to refuse the order. The order may well be bad, especially if it is to lie or do something illegal.

A good Leader should never require their Followers to do so, but many Leaders end up asking their employees to do just that and then use things like company loyalty as a way to encourage them to keep the secret or go along with the ruse.

Even if the order is not immoral, a Follower may have other reasons to not follow an order. As such, just because a Follower refuses to follow through on an order, you as Leader shouldn't immediately believe they are disloyal. Look at the order itself, and try to understand why they don't want to follow it. Or ascertain what problems the Follower has in the order itself, and perhaps there is a solution that can accommodate both of you.

However, the Follower may just be obstinate and not want to follow the order out of being disloyal. You need to determine if that is the case rather than presume it's the only reason for them to not follow orders.

Questioning What You Are Saying can be seen as disloyal and disrespectful. Many Leaders want to believe they are somehow above others, and to be questioned in any way is to be told they are less of a person. Admittedly, no one likes to be questioned. We all want to believe we are right, and if someone questions us, then we are inclined to defend our position at all costs, even if we can be logically proven that we are wrong, we may well defend ourselves as a matter of principal.

Just because a Follower does this, doesn't mean they are being disloyal. They might be, or they might be loyal to the point that they want you to be the best Leader you can be. Just like failure and the question of why, use this as an opportunity to improve yourself.

This can be a sign of disloyalty if the Follower does this often and seems to question as an act of defiance. Take careful steps to determine if this is the case, by observing their behavior over time rather react to things as they happen.

Having A Difference of Opinion may be an extension of questioning you. Since Followers now believe they are equal to their Leaders, they will have their own opinion, and thus are likely to be different to yours.

Just because a Follower has a different opinion than you, doesn't mean they disrespect your opinion. It simply means they think differently than you. Having an opinion that is different is not a sign of disloyalty because they don't just accept whatever premise you may have. It's the differences in the team that can make a team better, as chances are good that someone will think of something others overlook.

Just like questioning you, having a difference of opinion may be a sign of disloyalty if the Follower does so as a means to disagree with you at every turn.

Talking Behind Your Back definitely seems like a great betrayal, and thus it seems that they are disloyal to you. It may well be an act of disloyalty but remember that everyone needs to vent and there are some things you are not meant to hear. You are their boss, and as such, there is a level of separation from you to them. This separation means that when you push them to do their best, they can get frustrated and have a need to do what they can to not be frustrated, and your Followers might say and do something that they wouldn't do with you watching.

Just because a Follower talks behind your back, doesn't make them disloyal. In fact, they are likely quite loyal. All of us at one time or another talk about a friend or a loved one behind their back, and have a good laugh at their expense. It doesn't mean you like that person any less (though in some circumstances, it may), it simply means that you said something in an attempt to have a good time that you wouldn't otherwise say. This is no different than your Followers doing it to you and is by no means an automatic sign of disrespect.

By no means am I saying this is appropriate behavior and encourage you to do it, but understand it happens and the best thing you can do is let your Followers do it when they need to. Nor should you spy on them to find out what they are saying. If, however, someone reports to you that they are actively encouraging others to undermine you, then that is a cause for concern. It's one thing to get your frustrations out; it's another to completely disregard your authority.

Now that we've talked about disloyalty, and how to handle what might seem to be elements of it, let's talk about loyalty itself. A hundred years ago, you had loyalty simply because you had your own office and had a fancy title in front of your name. These days, you have to earn respect and loyalty, and must constantly do so. While this seems to be an annoyance, it is necessary as so many others have abused this privilege of automatic loyalty.

The following are things you can actively to gain loyalty of your Followers:

Set the Example

Rules are set for a reason. Often for safety, but more often for productivity. You require your Followers to follow the rules that are set by the company. Many Leaders and Managers feel that their position makes them above the rules, and can just break them. These rule-breaking Leaders might be quick to chastise their Followers for breaking the same rules, but seem so blase when they do so.

A great Leader is one who leads by example. Anything they require of their Followers, they themselves adhere to. They practice what they preach.

A Follower who sees a Leader break the rules that they themselves must adhere to in fear of losing their jobs, will themselves be less loyal to their boss on the principle they believe that their Leader thinks themselves above the rules. This goes back to being Intentional, and if you want your Followers to think so low of you, this is an excellent way to do so.

It is not fair to ask of others what you are not willing to do yourself.

-Eleanor Roosevelt

Commit to your Commitments

When you set an expectation, it needs to be followed through. Obviously, things come up that may well prevent you from doing so. This often means that you should be careful about what you promise to your Followers, or that when you make a promise, you give more realistic expectations.

Often times it is not an outside force that keeps your promises from fulfillment, rather it is the Leader lacking the commitment. When you make a promise to your Followers, then you must do everything you can to meet that expectation.

Even if you cannot get it done, it is important for your Followers to see or to know that you did what you could. The more you let down on your commitments for your Followers, the more likely they will have disloyalty to you. The more you can keep your word, the more they will want to do what they can to return the favor.

Even if you do fail, you can maintain their loyalty by doing what you could for them. It is not an all or nothing situation when it comes to your word, and Followers understand the concept of bureaucracy, but it is their Leader that helps them get what they need for the Followers to do their jobs better, whether that is new equipment, extra vacation days, or even a raise.

Unless commitment is made, there are only promises and hopes... but no plans.
-Peter Drucker

Use Failure, Not Scapegoats

This is a call back to the chapter: *Failure is an Option.*

When failure occurs, companies do like to try to find a scape-goat to avoid finding problems within the way they do things. This means that a Follower is likely to be blamed and possibly fired, telling all other Followers that they are simply expendable, and they shouldn't try any harder than they have to, in order to not stand out. Nothing creates disloyalty faster than Followers who believe they are a means to an end and can be sacrificed so those higher-ups can make a profit.

Read the chapter if you've not done so, but when failure happens, it is best to learn from it and use it as a tool to improve things, and not be in denial about it. Especially when you seek the Followers to contribute their input towards a solution.

> *Unintelligent people always
> look for a scapegoat.*
> -Ernest Bevin

Acknowledge Successful Followers

Everyone wants recognition for their work. Followers espec-ially want that, and in many ways need it. They need to know that their efforts are appreciated. Certainly, Leaders shouldn't recognize Followers who are doing what they should already be doing, at least not every second of every day, but when a Follower does something above and beyond, this should be acknowledged.

Followers who work hard and get little recognition will be dissatisfied for those they work for and be less inclined to work as hard in the future. A Follower who pushes themselves and get acknowledgment for their work is likely to try to do so again.

> ### *Correction does much, but*
> ### *encouragement does more.*
> -Johann Wolfgang von Goethe

Be Their Boss, Not Their Friend

Very few want to be the boss who is always a tyrant and cares little for their Followers. Leaders need not be a tyrant to their Followers, but there is a danger of being so personable, that you are instead their friend than their boss.

Trying to be their colleague will often result in your Followers trying to get away with something and you give into them. Doing so once will result in them wanting it again, and not doing it a second or third time can lead to disloyalty towards you.

This can be similar to the idea of not receiving gifts from clients or other entities you do business with. Accepting a gift can set a precedence that you may be required to do something in return, and can complicate future dealings. This is why companies make such strict policies on how to receive gifts. Like this, being friends with your Followers run the same risk, and it is better to let them know you are their Leader, not their friend.

This is not to say you can't be helpful to your Followers, but it's important that your generosity comes as their Leader and not their buddy.

With employees, customers, or clients: be friendly... not friends.

Richard S. George

Give Loyalty

You and your Followers are a team. What one of you do, affects the other. More importantly, if you desire to receive loyalty, you must therefore give loyalty. If you cannot be loyal to your Followers, then why should they be loyal to you?

You need to be there for your Followers and work to help them when they need it and be their advocate for anyone above you when their work or future is at stake. If you can show that you are there for them, and you won't leave them behind when the opportunity arises, thus showing them loyalty, they are likely to give the same loyalty in return, if not more so.

Understand that there are a lot of bad Leaders out there. Every one of us has had a bad Leader at least once in our career. They often lack loyalty to their Followers, as they can be self-interested in their own needs and fail to consider their Follower's needs because they don't have to. Why give this Leader any loyalty when they refuse to give any?

You need to be the Leader your Followers need, but they won't be so quick to give you Loyalty, likely out of bad past experiences. In order for them to give you the loyalty needed for the job to get done, you must give them loyalty first.

I can't expect loyalty from the Army if I do not give it.

-George C. Marshall

IS COMMUNICATION AN AUTOMATIC TRANSFER?

The short answer: no.

> *People fail to get along because*
> *they fear each other; they fear*
> *each other because they don't*
> *know each other; they don't know*
> *each other because they have not*
> *communicated with each other.*
> -Dr. Martin Luther King Jr.

Probably the only business subject written about as often as Leadership is communication. In many cases, they are the closely linked. If you can make someone understand what you are trying to accomplish, how to do it, and why it must be done, you will be both an effective communicator and an effective Leader.

Communication is not linear, nor simple. It's not always possible to see what can go wrong or to prevent it. If Leadership is the treasure map to success and happiness, communication is the metaphoric quicksand which hides around every corner, threatening to pull you into the quagmire.

The single largest mistake we make in communicating is that we assume what we said is what the other person heard. Certainly, you can recall being frustrated because you gave instructions which were clear, unmistakable, impossible to misunderstand... yet, somehow it was.

In management classes, we are taught that the method for ensuring this does not happen is to receive feedback. Oh, if only it were so simple! Feedback is necessary, sure, but feedback is another form of communication which can easily be derailed, and for the same reasons.

I have developed the **Transactional Model For Communication**, which gives you some idea of everywhere the message can be misunderstood...

TRANSACTIONAL MODEL OF COMMUNICATION

The single largest mistake we make in communicating is that we assume what we said is what the other person heard, especially feedback.

As you can see, the basic "send-receive-feedback model" is woefully inadequate to help us understand everything that goes into even the simplest communication. The Transactional Model gives you a map for diagnosing when and where a communication may have gone wrong. Much the way you need to know the inner workings of a combustion engine before you can diagnose a car problem, you must understand the inner workings of communication before you can diagnose a communication issue.

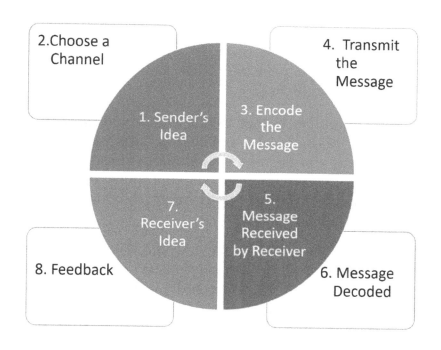

Communication – the human connection – is the key to personal and career success.

-Paul J. Meyer

Let's walk through the steps in the **Transactional Model of Communication**:

1. **SENDER'S IDEA** – This is where communication starts. This is what you want to say and the idea you want to get across, whether as a request, suggestion, input, or a command.

   This is the easiest part of the process, because **you know what you want to say**. It starts with a synapse firing in your brain that leads to an abstract picture – it is an idea.

   The problem is that this is where you have to slow down, take a breath, and be introspective. You need to know if you need or should communicate this message, and if so: how you will communicate it (see #2). Remember that some thoughts should remain just that, thoughts.

2. **CHOOSE A CHANNEL** – The next question that you need to decide is how will you deliver this message? In face-to-face communication, there is the power of watching body language, of immediate feedback, and of the ability for the back-and-forth of conversation. Face-to-face verbal communication remains the most effective communication channel.

   Phone communication allows for some of this, but it doesn't allow you to perceive body language. While a phone call is easier than face-to-face communication, if you are met with a hectic day (as is bound to happen), then even immediate phone contact may be difficult.

Voice communication (ie, face-to-face, phone, video chat) may not be an option, and in some ways may be an inadequate form of communication. Likely, the only time voice may be inadequate is when there is complex instruction, which then written communication becomes necessary. This may be a letter, an email, or even a text message (for a shorter message).

You want to choose the channel which gives you the best venue for transferring information, but also one which you can reliably ensure the message will be received. The options for choosing a channel are growing every day.

For this message I want to convey to you today I have chosen to write it in this book. It could have been an online video, a podcast, a seminar, a TED Talk, a blog post, a social media post... every day, the list of communication method grows.

3. **ENCODE THE MESSAGE** – Now that we know the message and have chosen the channel, we must choose how to encode that abstract picture into the words. We must intentionally choose to add any other data to help clarify our point:
   - Is this a request or a command?
   - Is it a plea for support or a warning about dangers?
   - Are you basing your message on logic or emotion?

This book could spend page upon page just discussing the intricacies of encoding a message. What we all should know is that words, tone, and facial expressions matter. When we encode the message, we must be aware of all of the "meta-data" and the noise and filters that our message may be subjected to.

4. **TRANSMIT THE MESSAGE** – Finally it is time to transmit the message. We must be vigilant and diligent to ensure that the delivery of our message does not convey any other data to the receiver than what we intend for them to receive. We may include:

- Body language, facial expressions, hand gestures
- The way we dress
- Tone of our voice, emphasis on certain words, volume of voice
- The pace at which we speak
- Time of day we give the message
- How we format a message (ie, written)
- How we address the receiver (use of last name versus first name)
- If we address one-on-one (versus a group)

As I said, we could spend many pages on the different ways in which we can encode and transmit our message. The things listed above, when added to simply our words, can have an enormous effect on the message that we are trying to communicate. The question: is it enhancing or distracting?

Let's take a moment here and look at the top half of the **Transactional Model of Communication**. More specifically, let us look at #4. One of the things we mentioned was emphasis. Below is a simple message, "I didn't say Rich was stupid." Looking at this sentence, think about how using different emphasis on each of the words individually might alter the meaning of that statement. In fact, I have written out each word emphasized, and I want you to read it aloud, apply the emphasis to each bolded (and italicized) word.

I didn't say Rich was stupid.
(Someone else might have.)

I *didn't* say Rich was stupid.
(Someone thought I said it.)

I didn't *say* Rich was stupid.
(I might think it, but I didn't say it.)

I didn't say *Rich* was stupid.
(I said someone was stupid, just not Rich.)

I didn't say Rich *was* stupid.
(I likely said he is stupid)

I didn't say Rich was *stupid*.
(What I said might not have been flattering, but I didn't say stupid.)

In how many of these statements is Rich actually stupid?

Once we have sent the message, so many of us think that communication is complete, but in reality, we've only just begun. This is where we have sent the message and where we can lose control of the same message. Now it is up to those that receive the message to control the mechanics of communication.

Now let's pivot to the bottom half of the **Transactional Model of Communication,** to discuss what happens to the message that we have sent. These are simply additional areas where breakdowns can and do occur.

5. **MESSAGE RECEIVED BY RECEIVER** – In this stage the receiver accepts and perceives all the metadata: they receive the sounds, the sights, everything that the five essential senses can pick up. You have chosen the right channel for your needs, and the receiver has taken possession of the message.

69

Are you sure?

You must remember that just because a message was sent does not mean that a message was received, nor does it mean that the same message sent is what was received.

6. **MESSAGE DECODED** - Now the receiver hears, or sees your message in its raw form. They will run it through a series of personal filters:

   - What they think the message will say before they read it
   - Or what they think is being said as they hear it
   - Their level of intelligence and education
   - Any bias they might have

   Add to the top of all of that with any distraction occurring in their head or their environment at the moment.

   The message can be completely clear and obvious, but once it has been through the blender of being decoded by the receiver, will it look anything like what you sent?

   In our earlier example of whether Rich was stupid or not, the receiver must tangle with their own ideas about what they thought they heard – which they might be influenced by what they personally think of Rich – in order to determine what their idea will be.

7. **RECEIVER'S IDEA** – The receiver now decides what you transmitted and it results in an idea or abstract picture in their head. They now have a synapse that has fired.

Now, what are the chances that the abstract picture that you had in your head is identical to the picture that is in the receiver's head?

I am writing this book with the hopes that millions of people will read it; can I be certain that you as the reader know with clarity what I am trying to convey?

9. **FEEDBACK** – The only way to ensure alignment in communication is to engage in thoughtful feedback with those that you communicate with. Knowing that someone "listened" to you is not only conveyed by their ability to parrot back the words that you said, but to layer in the emotional, logical, and intent of your message. To know the intent of one's message is true listening.

In many ways, the message process now starts all over again, with their feedback starting the process at step one and is their process of communicating to you through Transactional Model of Communication.

One way to look at good communication is for all parties to acknowledge and understand each other's message, even if that starts as new information or feedback. Comparing the two, feedback can also suffer the same pitfalls and detours as the initial conversation that initiated the need for feedback.

When I think about what can go wrong in communication, I shudder to think about how many times in just the past week that I have been misunderstood, or that I have misunderstood people in my life.

No one would talk much in society if they knew how often they misunderstood others.

-Johann Wolfgang von Goethe

Think about the Telephone game we played as children. One person speaks into another person's ear giving a message, and the next person is meant to relay that message to the next person. More often than not, the final person reveals a message completely different than the original. The first person likely said it clear as day, but then whispering would not be an effective means of transmitting a message. More than that, it helps demonstrate the breakdown of communication that so often occurs.

An example of communication in a business environment is that a client meeting has been changed from 9am to 8am. Now say that you must communicate to your business partner, what ways can you do that, and what can go wrong?

- Leave a voicemail
  - No guaranteed it is heard.
  - Might be interference during recording
  - Accidently deleted
  - Cell service goes down
  - They're out of their service area
- Send a text message
  - Information suffers from autocorrection
  - There might be a delay in delivery
  - Phone could be off
- Send an email
  - Same problems as voicemail and text message
  - Might get so many emails it gets lost in the Inbox
  - Might go to Spam filter
  - They might infer additional communications "between the lines"

- Face-to-Face interaction
  - Might be too busy now to see you
  - They had a lot on their plate and easily forget
  - They forgot to write it down

The point of this is not to say that communication is not worth doing. Certainly, if you need a business partner to show up an hour early, and they arrived at 8:30am, still believing the meeting is at 9am, they are now a half an hour late for the meeting.

Whose responsibility is that?

It really depends on how you tried to communicate with said person. If you only tried one method, despite its importance, you share a lot of that responsibility. If you tried multiple methods of communication, even if it comes off as annoying, and they are still late, then the responsibility falls entirely on them.

With communication, the total possible problems that can occur is essentially endless. Even this chapter on communication contains dangers:
- Will you understand the examples given?
- Have the steps been adequately described?
- Do you grasp the intended message that communication is a complex structure which should not be taken for granted?
- Is there a typo in the chapter which catches your eye and distracts you from the message because you now sense a lack of professionalism in the writing?
- Why won't that dog across the street stop barking while you're trying to read?!?

The kicker to communication is that people may interpret our inflection of certain words, even if it is not there, especially with written communication, inferring additional meaning. This can be an element of Hindsight Bias, in that people remember what they heard or read differently than what was actually written or said. Are we then responsible for their interpretations?

We may not have had any emphasis on any specific word and spoke as straight as possible... yet people infer a meaning "between the lines". The important thing to remember is that while we are not responsible for how people interpret our words, we are responsible for making sure they have the proper understanding in the face of communication as a whole.

As we discuss throughout this book so far, consider that ideas cannot be "given" to another person. They can be offered as a set of data, encoded and transmitted through a channel, and then run through a complex set of filters, but ultimately the receiver can design or devise their own idea.

Like the adage about the horse that has been led to water, you cannot force anyone to drink your idea. They have led a different life than you have; therefore, your message must travel their path, and you must do everything you can to make sure your idea, your message, has survived the trip and is firmly grounded in the receiver's brain.

Ultimately, Leadership is communication. When we see communication as a passive process that involves releasing something from our sphere of influence onto someone else, merely believing that because we said it others must have it, then we're rolling the dice... and as anyone who has ever been to a casino knows, the odds are not with you.

Just as mechanics need to understand how an internal combustion engine works or a doctor must understand how the heart relates to the lungs and the brain, they must first understand the relationship of the components to diagnose what is failing. We as Leaders must understand the mechanics of communication before we can diagnose what is going wrong within our communication.

As Leaders, we must communicate with clarity. Clarity that is crystal clear, high definition, 1080p, 4K ultra HD. We need to be Intentional, and be present when we strive to have meaningful interactions with our Followers.

THINKING OF COMMUNICATION AS A PASSIVE ONE-WAY PROCESS IS LIKE GAMBLING...

THE ODDS ARE NOT GOOD

PART II – THE PIECES: THE TWELVE "C'S"

As a Manager, the habits I learned and processes to which I became addicted have enabled me to thrive. I am a voracious reader, I am addicted to pursuing knowledge, and I love making difficult situations simple. Leadership can be difficult and I continue to strive for its simplicity. Throughout my years of Leadership, I have diligently tried to isolate the characteristics of good Leaders. Many business books and ideological philosophies gave great insight to my quest, yet the real test was practicality and simple implementation.

I created my C-list of the Leadership characteristics to which I believe are the foundational characteristics or attributes that an effective Leader must forever be thoughtful and aware of in their day-to-day lives. I have spent most of my adult life watching these attributes in other Leaders such as politicians, CEO's, parents, and religious leaders, and just those that have been influencers in my life. Each of these characteristics are derived and learned from my career experiences and each is both practical and simple.

COURAGE

Take a position, even when it is painful.

Courage is the most important of all the virtues, because without courage, you can't practice any other virtue consistently.
-Stedman Graham

If one "C" could be said to be the most important, it is **Courage**.

Many politicians and management instructors will suggest that a person should never take a position or shape because that makes it more difficult to become a target; that not taking a position is safer. In fact, Robert Greene in the *"48 Laws of Power"* revealed the 48th law of power as: Assume Formlessness. By taking a shape, by having a visible plan, you open yourself to attack, which is something a powerful person shouldn't have.

While refusing to take a position is safe... it is **NOT** Leadership. A Leader, by the nature of their actions, presents themselves for accountability. They don't avoid it, they don't try to straddle the fence in case fortunes fall one way or the other. A Leader has the Courage to take a position and say, "This is what I believe."

In my book *"Hire the Best Ditch the Rest"* I describe a scenario of an employee named Jim, and my anxiety regarding whether he should be fired. Terminating an employee can be, for many people, one of the most stressful tasks of a Leader. I explain that to have the Courage to meet this task, I ask myself how I would feel if I learned this morning that Jim had given his notice. What would be my reaction?

Of my possible reactions, I came up with three:
- I would either be upset
  - In which case firing Jim would be bad idea
- I would be relieved
  - In which case firing Jim is a good idea
- I would be indifferent
  - In which case firing Jim is certainly not a bad choice

Once I could internalize my own feelings, once I knew what position I supported, then I could have the Courage to take a position publicly and have the Courage to talk to Jim. Courageous conversations as a Leader are critical!

> *I learned that courage was not the absence of fear, but the triumph over it. The brave man is not he who does not feel afraid, but he who conquers that fear.*
>
> -Nelson Mandela

Courage is not recklessness. Courage is not indifference to the consequences. Courage is not rushing blindly into the battle zone without any concern for coming out alive. That's not Courage; that's stupidity.

Many consider Courage to be a trait, something you either have or don't have. In truth, Courage is a skill, and it is something you must learn to have, something that takes practice by facing your fear and not letting it hold you back.

Courage is the ability to take a position, one which you can understand, defend, and communicate, and be willing to stand by that choice. Unless of course evidence tells you that you must change the position. In fact, it takes even more Courage to acknowledge when we are wrong. This is one of the ways in which to use failure to your benefit.

> *A coward dies a thousand times before his death, but the valiant taste of death but once. It seems to me most strange that men should fear, seeing that death, a necessary end, will come when it will come.*
> -William Shakesphere

In our actions, of course, death is not the result we will face, but metaphorically, accountability can result in defeat, the death of our success, and the death of our goals. The Leader takes a position and dares defeat to wrestle success from their grasp. An effective Leader finds the will to be courageous in all that they do and the drive to be accountable.

To practice Courage, you can do the following:

- **Follow Your Gut**
  Sometimes the best decision is the tried and true way, of what has been done before. Sometimes however, it requires a person to be brave and venture into the unknown, in order for things, and companies, to move forward.

  Creators of Google were met with the task of Courage. They knew that a dedicated search company was the way to go, and many scoffed at their idea. Despite the challenges, they continued on. Can you imagine a world without Google?

  Following your gut is risky, as it should be. There's a chance you can be wrong. Be aware of that, and take that fear into account. If you have no fear in following your gut, then following it is not an act of Courage, and the idea may not ultimately matter. You may tell others you're not afraid, but some part of you is... it's OK to be afraid. Take that into account when it comes to what your gut says, and have the Courage to do it, or have the Courage not to.

- **Make the Tough Calls**
  Many would-be leaders would delegate the responsibility in making the tough decisions or even giving bad news. Someone has to do it, and they would rather protect their reputation than to follow through on a decision.

  A Leader must not be afraid to make the tough call. Whether it is making a decision that could fire half your staff, a cut in pay, or giving bad news... you as a Leader must do it. You won't win any popularity contests, but then one doesn't become a Leader to be liked.

- **Take and Address Feedback/Criticisms**
  No one likes to hear anything negative about themselves. Many will do everything they can to avoid it. Yet, those individuals will never improve if they don't hear the ways in which they fail, and take the opportunity to improve. We've discussed this throughout the first part of this book, whether it is using failure or utilizing effective communication.

- **Stay the Course**
  When you make a decision for a project, sometimes the project may not live up to initial expectations. In light of this, many may escape from the project for the fear of failure, or to be looked upon negatively.

  It takes Courage to see something through, and you've got to ask yourself if there is still good that can emanate from continuing the project, even if what you initially set out to do is no longer a possibility.

  This goes back to the Law of Attraction, that just because there is a hiccup along the way, doesn't mean the project is doomed to fail, and if you believe it is, then perhaps all your project will fail.

- **Know When to Walk Away**
  So far, in practicing Courage, I've stated that you've got to Stay the Course when things don't meet your expectations. I also said Follow Your Gut, and if you feel that a project needs to stop and you move onto something else – and not just because of a few hiccups, but you know deep down it is the right course of action – then listen to your gut, accept failure, and walk away from it.

  Running away from your problems is easy, but quitting when you've given your all, that's a challenge that takes actual Courage to do.

Risk is part of the game if you want to sit in that chair.

-James T. Kirk, Star Trek: Generations (1994)

- **Take Risks**

  Kirk was talking about the captain's chair, a great position of Leadership easily recognized in our culture today, even if fictional. In the moment he said those words, he was speaking of having Courage to do what needs to be done, especially when it meant taking a risk for a greater good.

  It also seems to go without saying that to be successful in business, one must take risks. As we said in this book, rushing head-on into a battle blindly is stupidity. While it is a risk, it is not one you should just take on a whim. When you can, it is best to take a calculated risk.

  In taking a risk, it requires Courage to see it through, but it also takes Courage to actually do it. You can try to avoid risk in your career, but this creates stagnation. More than likely, those others who take risks are likely to move up in their careers. If you're OK with playing it safe and staying comfortable, that may be fine for you, but it also disqualifies you from being a Leader.

  Taking a risk is scary, but in order to have Courage, you must face that fear. Only then can you be a true Leader. And yes, you may fail, but failure is part of the learning process... so when you try to take a risk again, learn from what you did before to make better decisions.

As you continue with the 12 C's, remember to have Courage. While you may not need some pieces in your quest to be a better Leader, you always need to have Courage.

This also means that to be a good Leader, you will also have fear. It's strange to say, but it's true. A good Leader is not fearless... a good Leader knows how to channel their fear into a useful measure. How does a Leader do that? Courage.

The secret to happiness is freedom... And the secret to freedom is courage.
–Thucydides

CHARISMA

You must leverage your influence to get the job done.

There are people for whom Charisma comes naturally. There are people toward whom other people are naturally drawn, naturally trusted, and naturally followed. Many of us look at people who we see as naturally charismatic and feel a twinge of jealousy: If only I could have that!

These are rarities; these are not the measuring stick we should use. Charisma can be a learned behavior, and everyone can improve their influence on others. Yes, there is an element of nature to it, and we all have our limits, but it is also a matter of nurture, of learning, and most of all... passion. **Charisma is the direct result of passion**.

My friend Steve is by most accounts an easy-going, non-intrusive, at times almost invisible guy. People like him, but mostly because he doesn't offend anyone and doesn't intrude on anyone's day. He is not, by all measures, a charismatic man.

However, if you get Steve to talk about his garden, he becomes a different person. His expression changes, his eyes light up, his posture straightens, he becomes more animated, his words have power, and before long, you are caught up in the excitement of a subject that for many people is a step above unconsciousness, at best. Steve becomes charismatic and can make you see the things that he sees in what he enjoys... because he is passionate about it. He finds his Charisma, and he is unstoppable.

When people lack Charisma, often they lack passion for what they are doing. Don't think of Charisma as a gift, as something you simply have. Again, there are people like that, but they are rare. If you cannot find the passion for what you do, for the team that you lead, then you will not find your Charisma.

When you find your passion you find your Charisma, and you will discover that people will react to your passion, they will feed off your energy, and they will find that they want to share in it. You will influence people, you will get more decisions made in your favor, you will lead your team with greater success, because you will become that person people want to like, and to be like – passionate and charismatic. People will work harder for you, and they might not always know why; they will want to. That is the power of Charisma.

> *Being a Leader gives you charisma. If you look and study the Leaders who have succeeded, that's where charisma comes from, from the leading.*
> -Seth Godin

Like many skills, practice makes perfect. Just finding your passion in a project is not enough if you are not naturally a charismatic person. As rare as it is to be naturally charismatic, transforming Charisma from passion instantaneously is practically impossible.

Below are some things you can do to turn passion into Charisma:

- **Confidence**

  As strange as this might sound, this will likely will be your best tool to implement Charisma, "Fake it till you make it". A key aspect of Charisma is confidence itself. If you sound confident in what you're saying, then you appear passionate about what you're doing, and with passion comes Charisma.

  To be confident, you must have a strong sense of what you're doing and who you are. This goes back to being Intentional and the Laws of Attraction. If you exude confidence, then others around you will be confident.

  In order to do this, you must leave your problems at the door, and any self-doubt you might have, vanish once you are at work. You don't want your Followers slacking off their work because of a personal problem, and you as a Leader must lead by example.

  If you need to, practice what you will say to your Followers before you say it. They recommend this before you speak to your own boss, but this can help with your own Followers. Practice the night before, and try to anticipate questions they might have. Try to speak with authority without being overpowering.

- **Optimism**
  While it helps to be a realist about how you conduct business, one should be optimistic when they interact with their Followers. Optimism can inspire the world, and when you have an optimistic view towards your work, it shows your passion.

  Of course, we are not talking of unrealistic optimism, of saying something is good even when you know it is bad. However, when taking a risk or asking people to give a lot to a project, having an optimistic approach can help. This can help especially with the Law of Attraction and even help to lead through elements of failure.

  If you show optimism, your Followers are likely to embrace optimism, and even if your optimism turns out wrong and you are met with failure, then you can embrace said failure towards your future endeavors.

> ### *Being positive in a negative situation is not naive. It's leadership.*
> -Ralph Marston

- **Communication**
  We've talked extensively about the Transactional Model of Communication, and if for any reason you skipped that chapter (the last one of Part I: *Is Communication an Automatic Transfer*), then I strongly urge you to read it. Communication is very important, not just to get your message across, but for people to feel they are being heard and that they are a part of the conversation.

How easy is it for people in a position of power to railroad their Followers by talking over them and not letting them get a word in edgewise? This might well be passion, but it takes away from Charisma, at least for those that must be your Followers. Likely they will grow to spite you, and no amount of Charisma can overcome that.

This concept is more discussed in Leading and/or Managing, as it is the role of the Manager to get the work done, but it is the Leader to inspire the Followers. Communication is the key difference here, in that both have a different method in how they accomplish what needs to be done. Managers can be Charismatic, but Leaders **must** be Charismatic.

However, as great as it is to have Charisma, there is a danger to it as well that can affect your effectiveness as a Leader. Having Charisma is not just a tool to get your Followers to do their job or a simple manipulation technique to be well-liked, it can also be a drug that can be abused.

Having Charisma can be addicting when you realize that your behavior makes you popular and gets the work done. If you treat it like a drug and only employ it when you need something, your Followers will quickly figure that out. Don't underestimate the intelligence of your Followers. They may see you when you don't realize it, and every company will have its own rumor mill.

Charisma requires confidence building, and while too little takes away from passion; too much can make for an egotistical Leader. An egotistical Leader cares just for themselves, and while that show passion and cause them to be Charismatic, it is shallow and empty, especially for the Followers who must follow.

To avoid this, this requires perhaps the most important aspect of Charisma: self-awareness. This gets into the next C of Character, but you must ask yourself how you are perceived by your Followers, and not ask it as a matter of popularity, but one of effectiveness.

This can be difficult when we consider the Dunning-Kruger effect, as mentioned in *A Leader Must Be Intentional*. Those that build their self-identity around their self-confidence tend to think higher of their abilities than their actual capabilities, often because they are too biased to see their flaws. Too much Charisma can cause this, which requires a level of humility mixed with Charisma to keep yourself in check to be an effective Leader.

Be who you need to be
for your Followers.

CHARACTER

It's not written in your DNA, but it is who you are at your core; it is your default position. Know yourself: Assess, Evaluate, and Correct.

We are influenced by the events of the day, by the actions of the people around us, by our fears, and by our distractions. Each of these influences factors into our own behavior, and they can have a negative as well as a positive influence. A Leader doesn't try to excuse a bad choice by claiming it was a bad day; that is not Leadership behavior. Knowing who you are at your core is critical to Leadership.

Character comes in the form of who we are deep down inside. Think of it as your inner core. As we interact with the world from birth, we develop a wall (or an outer shell). Our outer shell is what people see. Ideally, our inner core and outer shell speak to each other, and as our outer shell gets more involved, it relies on our inner core to remain true to who we are.

93

In a way, our outer shell is an ambassador to our inner core to the rest of the world. Unfortunately, our outer shell can become corrupted by the influence of the world around us and ignore who we are on the inside, ignore our Character. When this happens, we must return to our default position.

Think of calling the help desk when you have a computer problem; most often you are asked to restart your computer and start in Safe Mode. Safe Mode, for all intents and purposes, is your computer's default position – because this is when your computer operates at its best.

Safe Mode only uses what is necessary for the computer to run, unlike when you normally go into Windows with extra processes running in the background by default. From Safe Mode, a computer technician can help troubleshoot a computer, as this tests how a computer should work without all the extra bells and whistles.

Just like the computer, you must know where your default position is, and when a problem arises, be able to bring yourself to your Safe Mode, or default position.

It would be impossible to never be impacted by the events, people, and conditions in your life. Everything from a minor argument with your significant other to the common cold, or worse the severe illness of a loved one or fear of something down the road, can impact your behavior. You are human.

Having Character does not mean you are invulnerable to outside elements; it means you constantly assess how conditions have affected your behavior, assess your current behavior, evaluate that behavior, and adjust your behavior to its default position in order to correct it.

The thing with the 12 C's, is that the majority of them deal with how you interact with your business and your Followers, but Character is one that requires you to evaluate not only how you interact with your Followers and your job, but to the world around you, especially when you don't think anyone can see you, or believe that no one will know of your actions.

There are many guides out there about how to develop your Character and a lot of keywords associated with that. Perhaps it is the United States Air Force that has the most succinct list of how to build your Character, that I have adapted for use in this book. Note that there are a lot of ways to maintain character, but the following three is the bare minimum you need to be a good Leader.

- **Integrity First**
  Integrity is about commitment to doing the right thing at all times. Not just because it can lead to a good outcome, which it sometimes doesn't, but because it is the right thing to do. This becomes difficult as the business world is cut-throat, and it seems that you must sleeze your way to the top. As difficult as a competitive career can be, there is still room for having integrity as a Leader.

  Followers look to their Leaders for integrity. They often consider it one of the most important attributes in their Leaders. Since this is the 12 C's and not the 12 I's, integrity falls under Character. Being ethical and fair are desired traits for Leaders, but it is too easy to cheat others along the way, and that has a way of catching up with you eventually.

  As a Leader, your words, actions, promises, and decisions have a profound effect on your Leaders and your Followers. Again, be Intentional in what you do, and put integrity at the top of our Character.

The most important persuasion tool you have in your entire arsenal is integrity.

-Zig Ziglar

- **Followers Needs Before Self**
  The US Air Force lists this as, "Service Before Self". Service refers to the Armed Services, or specifically the Air Force. In keeping that sentiment, I adapted it to being Followers Needs. As we discussed in Charisma, we must remember to put the needs of others above our own needs, and that includes the needs of our Followers.

  It's easy to say that we have higher authority, and thus deserve more. It's a slippery slope, because where does that end? Once we put ourselves above our Followers, our Leaders, and the business itself, then that leads to trouble. While you have authority as Leader, your authority is of service to your Followers, your Leaders, and the business. It might be strange to say, but remember that without Followers, then the vision of the Leader will never see the light of day.

- **Excellence In All You Do**
  This one is fairly straightforward. You must strive to always do your best in the projects you do and your role as Leader. Doing your best is a big reflection on your character. It taps into being Intentional, the Law of Attraction, and your Leadership Brand. Trust me when I say; Followers know when their Leaders put their best effort in, and when they phone it in.

Utilizing these three elements will help build and maintain your Character. There are other ways to develop and improve your Character, but when you need to reset, this is the Safe Mode of who you are. If you're not doing these three things, then fall back on these elements.

Resetting yourself is a tricky thing however, as the greatest enemy to Character is Justification. Those lacking in Character will often live their lives through Justification, that what they do must be done for some purpose that they themselves directly benefit from. Like taking an extra hour for lunch, when your Followers can get in trouble for not being back the very minute they need to. One could justify that their need to take more time is that they have more responsibilities. Going back to being Intentional, how does that look to your Followers?

Our characters are a result of our conduct.
-Aristotle

Poor Character often comes when those in a position of power believe they are above the rules that their Followers are set to follow. Of course, there are benefits to elevating to a position of power, and by no means should you deny yourself what you've earned. At the same time, just because you can circumvent the rules, doesn't mean you should.

Your evaluation of Character comes from the perception of others, and how they view your actions is a reflection of the dedication to their job. If they see you abusing your job, they themselves will do the same. Again, be Intentional.

So when productivity is down, and your Followers are not respecting you or doing their best, then perhaps you need to look at your own actions. As it was said in the 2000 film, Remember the Titans, "*Attitude reflects Leadership*", and if your Followers have a bad attitude, as much as it could be them as the problem, it may very well be a problem of Character of the Leader.

If this is the case, and it is your Character that is the problem, then you need to reset yourself to your Safe Mode – to your default position. We talked about what that looks like, but we must know how to be self-aware:

- **Mindfulness**
  A key step to resetting yourself, if not the first step, is to put yourself into the mind of how others perceive you. This is difficult if your Character is already corrupted, but not impossible. You need to look at your own actions and ask, "If I was one of my Followers, how might I feel about this?"

  It may also help to remember a time when you were a Follower, whether to your current boss or to a previous boss before you became a Leader. Remember who you are in those circumstances, then ask about your own actions.

  The key here is to be absolutely honest with yourself and avoid Justification. It's not about whether or not there is a valid reason for it, it's about how it looks.

  Your Followers may not know why you take the actions you do. In that case, ask yourself "If my Followers did know, would it affect them?" You need to care about how they feel in order to motivate them.

  If your reason for stepping around the rules a little was of benefit to the business, then you are in the clear. And you might not be able to tell them, but you can certainly hint that it was necessary.

  However, if your reason is entirely personal and of no benefit to anyone except you, then that is a time to reset yourself to your default position.

- **Weaknesses**

  This is hard for everyone to do. One of the general questions asked in an interview is, "Name a weakness you have". No one likes to reflect on what they do wrong, especially those whose lives focus on correcting the wrongs of others, such as a Leader to their Followers.

  This goes back to using failure, but instead of a direct failure as a result of your actions, this is a reflection of your failures over a long period of time. Now don't be afraid of the words "Failure" and "Weakness" at a time like this.

  It's important to know where you are lacking, and what you need to improve upon. It's one thing to reset to your default position, but what's the point of doing so if not to correct your behavior? It's like taking your computer to Safe Mode, think everything is fine, then go back to the regular mode of Windows, believing all is fine.

  Finding our own weakness is difficult, as we can use Justification in our actions, or simply lie to ourselves to feel better. It's what we do as humans. We don't want to feel bad, so we don't. This may require feedback from your Followers (though they may not be truthful on their boss's weaknesses in fear of reprisal) or an outside observer. Perhaps you can go to your boss or the HR department for an evaluation. If not them, then family and/or friends are likely your best option.

  When you can evaluate your weakness, then you can take yourself into your default position mentioned above, and build off of that to overcome the weaknesses you have as Leader.

Once you can do these two key steps, then you should be able to reset yourself to a default position, then engage the 3 core values of Character. From there, you can evaluate your life, identify where you want to go, and decide how to modify your Character to get you there.

Character is like a tree and reputation like a shadow. The shadow is what we think of it; the tree is the real thing.
-Abraham Lincoln

COMPASSION

The most profound human emotion, a desire to alleviate another's suffering.

Oftentimes, as Leaders and Managers, we are told to check our emotions at the door, that we must approach our decision-making process with cold detachment, in order to be objective. This is no way to live, and this is no way to lead.

While it may be easier to be cold in order to be objective, that kind of thinking is only a short-term solution to the productivity of your Followers. A long-term solution to their productivity is Compassion.

Whatever their skills, motivations, and purpose on our team, our Followers are people. Everything that influences your life – the people you love, the goals you have, your fears, doubts, and your desires – they have these, too.

In order to get the most productivity out of your Followers, you must get to know them, and understand who they are. It may not be possible or advisable to intimately know all your Followers, but you must be able to see them as individuals and know that part of being an effective Leader is taking their concerns and goals into account as much as your own.

In *What About Loyalty?*, we mentioned that Followers today no longer see themselves at the mercy of the company. Followers today see themselves as equal to their job and their Leaders. With this change in perspective amongst your Followers, so too do you as a Leader must change how you lead. Using Compassion is the way to do so.

Compassion, from a purely objective standpoint, can enable the Law of Attraction; if you're compassionate, then you're Followers are most likely to be compassionate. If as a Leader you show interest in your Followers and their needs, then your Followers may well do so for you as the Leader, to one another, and very likely to your customers (if your Followers have interaction with the customers).

A way to look at the use of Compassion as a Leader is a way of an Investment. You want your Followers to do well and to feel a part of something greater. However, if they feel that they are only seen as a grunt and a number on a spreadsheet when it comes time to pay their wages, they will be less inclined to give their best. By showing interest in your Followers, you are investing in their potential to do better.

Another key point from *What About Loyalty?* is to avoid being friends with your Followers. This is a tightrope to walk on: show just enough Compassion and concern for your Followers to feel validated, but not too much they think of you as their friend. At the end of the day, you are their boss, and you need them to respect you and take orders from you, as necessary.

If nothing else, understand the power of knowing your Follower's names. In his masterpiece, "How To Win Friends And Influence People", Dale Carnegie said, "Remember that a person's name is to that person the sweetest and most important sound in any language."

We all want to feel important, and when a true Leader knows who we are, we will. This is not intended as a ploy, though it has certainly been used as one; we must also remember the first principle that Carnegie outlined in that chapter: "Become genuinely interested in other people!"

Like many of the 12 C's, Compassion is a skill which requires active use to master. Below are a few building blocks to become a compassionate Leader:

- **Awareness**
  This really goes without saying, and yet many Leaders fail on this when they attempt to have Compassion. Just as this book often says Be Intentional, it is also important to Be Aware. Be aware of your Followers, be receptive to their needs as people, and most importantly, remember what those needs are.

- **Empathize**
  Don't just show you care... actually care. If they have something good to say in their lives, share that moment with them. Either relate to their experience with something in your life or ask them a few quest-ions. If it is something bad, show concern to them.

  However, as easy as it can be to fake this, I stress that you shouldn't fake it. Only give what you can actually give as a compassionate Leader. Perhaps you can't be that great Leader now, but with a little practice, you can.

- **Mindfulness**

  When it comes to making a decision, you're not always able to take your Follower's needs into consideration. It would be great if you could, but most often the decisions you must make can even work against your own needs and desires.

  However, there may come a time where a decision can be influenced by you considering different variables, and the Compassion for your Followers should be one of them. You are aware and have empathized with their concerns or lives in general, now is the time to take it to the next level and put their needs into the mix when it comes to making a decision.

  The best way to accomplish this is to put yourself in their shoes and try to understand how your decision will affect them. Perhaps the decision you make can't take their needs into full consideration, but knowing how they might be affected by a decision, means that you should know what to anticipate and develop a plan to make it easier on them with the decision is implemented.

- **Flexibility**

  It would be great if your Followers just did what they need to do and worked highly efficiently without any personal needs. Until we get robotic workers, we have to hire humans. Humans aren't always the most efficient workers, which is why you are their Leader, so you can lead them to do better.

  Unfortunately, many Leaders think little of their Followers and believe that they should just work and do nothing else. After all, that is what they are being paid to do. Followers have adapted to the changes in our world, and so too do Leaders need to adapt. Leaders need to become more dynamic in how they do their jobs, rather than be static in the old ways. A compassionate Leader is a Flexible Leader.

It's not to say that you must be flexible in every way as a Leader. Many things require stability and structure. However, some of the ways of old needs to be updated with the needs of today, and interaction with your Followers is one such way, and taking their concerns and work lives into consideration is another way. Open yourself up to new possibilities, and be flexible in how things can be done.

A nice indirect outcome from being more Compassionate is greater respect from your Followers. Even just remembering their name has a profound impact and can make a Follower's day. Add to that if you ask them about their day, or remember something about them. Followers want to work and do their best, but if they feel their Leader cares about them, they are likely to try a little bit harder, out of respect for their compassionate Leader.

I give warning here... don't use Compassion as a tool of manipulation. You might get away with it at first, and let your Followers believe you care, but the longer you act like you care, the more blowback it will cause when they find out that you don't. People want to be remembered, but if they learn that their compassionate Leader only showed Compassion as a way to use them, they will immediately lose respect for them and quite possibly decrease work productivity.

Believe me when I say that it is far easier to maintain rapport with actual Compassion, than to rebuild rapport after losing your Follower's trust and respect with false Compassion. Remember that we are all in this together. Treat your followers well because you want to treat them well, and you want them to feel needed.

Wisdom, compassion, and courage are the three universally recognized moral qualities of men.

-Confucius

CREATIVITY

**Leaders live outside the box.
Embrace change like it is your own
child.**

Leaders should always have the mentality of looking at how to do things better than they were done yesterday. Change is a necessity of business, and Leaders should embrace change as a means of survival, but should not embrace change because that is what is expected of them. To accomplish change requires innovation, and the key to innovation is Creativity, or rather, a creative mind.

The concept of change can be a scary one. We as humans shy away from change. We easily get comfortable with where things are, as we are often told, *"Don't fix what ain't broken"*. Unfortunately, we live in the future, a world where everyday something thought of as impossible now is very real. That comes at a great cost, that if you don't embrace it, you become a relic, you become extinct.

It's not enough to embrace ideas or to change as things come about. You have to take things a step further and innovate in anticipation of where things might go, rather than solve problems as you come upon them.

The concept of embracing change and creating new ideas cannot be overstated in your role as Leader. To survive in this world, we must embrace change, we must embrace innovation, **WE MUST EMBRACE CREATIVITY**, and the power it all brings to us and our Followers.

There are no boundaries to what can be accomplished, and no limitations to the roads that Creativity can take. As I travel the country and the world, I am constantly amazed at the artistic creations I have the privilege to see, and equally amazed at the solutions to complex and seemingly overwhelming business problems people face every day.

Of course, just because you can be inspired to do something differently each day, doesn't mean you should do it. As we mentioned in *Courage*, we shouldn't be indifferent to consequences. Meaning that with Creativity, it's good to think up ideas, but when you have an idea, do your research on it before implementing it.

Not all Creative ideas are good ideas.

If there is one thing I've learned in my life, is that innovation and novelty are required for progress. The problem becomes that maintaining the old way can often lead a business to become obsolete. They believe that the money they make now will always last, especially if they have done so for many years before.

Kodak is a good example of this. Kodak had a large market hold of inexpensive film for cameras, as well as cameras used for commercial enterprises, including filmmaking. Eventually, this company lost its place in the market.

In 1975, they invented the first digital camera, but didn't market it for fear of losing their photographic business, as they made a lot of money from film. In 1981, Kodak conducted a study on digital cameras and consumers and knew that eventually, consumers would transition to digital.

Instead of preparing for the change, they remained focused on selling more products, as that proved to work for them for nearly 100 years prior. In 2012, Kodak filed bankruptcy, as they got into the digital market too late.

This book, we talk a lot about change and Creativity, but we understand that sometimes, being creative can seem like a luxury. For many Leaders, they lack the time to be creative, especially depending on the business. Many of us work long hard hours trying to get projects done on time and putting out fires as they come. Then when we get a break from work, the last thing we want to do is to think about work. Usually, we want to relax and unwind, and prepare for the next day as best as we can.

To put it bluntly: No one said being a Leader was easy. We live in a very high-tech world, and while the demands are very real, so too is the Creativity required for a business to thrive. The key thing here that I am saying is that as a Leader, you must find time for Creativity, no matter how busy your life may be.

Creativity can come in strange ways, sometimes it can be a random thought that comes out of nowhere, or simply an idea that may have been sitting on the shelf. Despite the randomness of Creativity, this doesn't mean you can't set time for yourself each day to think about things.

Some look at that eureka moment as having first eliminated other ideas until that stroke of genius comes. Though, it is quite possible to structure your creativity to find that great idea, as your mind is already on business.

A good example of that eureka moment, and something we easily take for granted today, is the simple Post-It Note sticky. The Post-It Note was actually a glue accidentally invented by Dr. Spencer Silver, and then a product that sat around for years because no one could find a use for a really weak adhesive.

One day, Art Fry realized that the adhesive would be great for helping to keep his bookmark in place in his church hymnal, solving a frustrating problem he'd had with losing his place and his bookmarks. Suddenly, after five years sitting on the shelf, Post-It Notes became an overnight success.

Fear you may not have creativity? Today Creativity is a valued commodity, and we want to encourage children to hold onto their imaginations as long as possible, but certainly a few, from generations back, believed that good hard work was the only true way to rise above the rest. While hard work is good to have, a great creative brain on your shoulders can help you rise above the rest.

If you find you are lacking in Creativity, there are a few things you can do to enhance your creativity:

- **Tap All Resources**
  As a Leader, you have access to many different resources, from your leaders, to colleagues, to conferences, to even your own Followers. More than that, you have the Internet, which taps into knowledge from all over the world, from news stories to random ideas people have.

What enables Creativity is not one source having an idea, but usually several sources coming together. You'll often find that the next innovation solves a variety of problems, not just one by itself. Whether it is to improve an already existing item to giving the world something it never knew it needed, all of it starts with paying attention to the world around you.

- **Ask Questions**
  When you study the world around you, the next thing you must do is ask questions. Usually a 'What-if' question does the trick. You'll likely not have the answer, or if you do, the answer is preposterous. While you should try to answer the question, and take that to lead to a possible solution, a good way to workout your Creativity muscle is to think on what the answer could be.

  In this way, asking questions about the world around you in relation to your business is like lifting weights. Perhaps you want to be bench pressing your body weight, but you can't just start with that weight if you're out of shape. Just like you can't immediately come up with a brilliant answer if you lack in Creativity. Like both lifting weights and thinking creatively, working out is the way you get there, and for Creativiy, asking yourself questions and trying to answer them is your key to building muscle.

- **Collaborate**
  Perhaps you've come up with an idea, or you recognize a problem and only have half a solution. Collaboration can help take you to the next level. This can be a tricky one, especially if you have the potential for the next big innovation, you are quick to be distrustful of those who might take the idea for themselves.

Collaboration tends to be best if you have some good friends outside the company that you can rely on, provided that the idea can be discussed outside the company without breaking any rules/laws. If outside the company is not an option, try to coordinate with a few trusted people within the company.

Collaboration proves useful, as different minds often think in different ways, either because they are cut from a different cloth than you, or their life experiences have enabled them to see the world in a different way. Whatever the reason, take note on how they view the idea and where it leads them on input. This can enhance your creativity if you can learn to think in different ways, to help you look from new angles.

- **Practice the 12 C's**
  Perhaps the best way for you to become a creative Leader is to implement this book. A lot this book is about how to affect change in yourself to be a better version of you, or rather, be the best Leader that your Followers need.

  In being a better version of you, this allows you to tap into new areas of Creativity that you never knew you had. Embracing the 12 C's will allow you to reach new heights and see more of the world around you, and doing so will enhance your Creativity.

- **Distract Yourself**
  You can corral creativity, and try to designate a time and place for it, but quite often it is when our mind is idle that true creativity comes to us. It's not to say that you shouldn't still try to structure Creativity, as you definitely need to do so. Creativity in the business world often brings about solutions to problems or new ways of doing things.

Archimedes was given a task to determine if a crown from a goldsmith was made of pure gold or made of other metals. It was while taking a bath – a distraction – did he note how the water level rose with his body. This bout of creativity led to the conclusion that if he submerged the crown and the amount of gold it should have separately, then measure how much water each displaces, it could solve the problem of how to accurately determine if the crown was a fraud.

Many scholars doubt the accuracy of that story, but there is a lesson here, that sometimes stepping away can help lead us to innovation. This, of course, is not a solution to do all the time, but if you are ever lost in a problem, consider stepping away and relaxing. It doesn't always work, but sometimes a good relaxation can mean a fresh mind to look at the problem once more.

When we focus on a problem, the solution cannot manifest itself. Focus on solutions.

Creativity leads to innovation, and innovation leads to new ventures for your business. Leaders are known to have their vision, but unless that vision includes having the Creativity to make it happen, you are doomed to certain failure. See a problem, find a solution. Look at the world through the eyes of a child – see what others cannot see for fear of not conforming. Every day seek to gain a new perspective on life.

Creativity can be described as letting go of certainties.
-Gail Sheehy

COMPETENCE

**Surround yourself with the best
and you will be the best. Read
voraciously.**

You don't need to be the smartest person in the room, but as Leader, you do need to be clever. And the cleverest thing you can do is to surround yourself with smart people. You as Leader are the total sum of your Followers, and what they can do as a team is a reflection of you.

We often hear the term, 'Guilt By Association'. That applies here, but I prefer to call it 'Reflection By Association'. You are a reflection of what you Followers can do, and this spells out your Competence. If they are good people, you will be seen as a Good Leader. If they are smart, you're a Smart Leader. If they are bad and dishonest, I'm sure you can see where I'm going with this.

Many Leaders decry this as being unfair, but most of them do so when their Followers are not that great to begin with, especially if they did have a good team and now are reassigned to a bad team. They rested on the laurels of what their team was able to do on their own, taking credit for their effort as if their own, until they were given another team and it was shown what a bad Leader they actually are.

No such thing as bad student... only bad teacher.

-Mr. Miyagi, Karate Kid (1984)

Your Competency as a Leader comes when your team is at their best. If you can choose your team and hire who you need, then you want to surround yourself with the best and the brightest. However, you don't always get to choose your team, and this is where your competency comes into play. You must work your team to be the best it can be. After all, this is why you are a Leader, why you are put into this position. If Followers could do their best on their own, you wouldn't be needed. However, you are in your position, and the competency of your job is having the best team you can possibly have.

It's fair to say that all of the 12 C's are interlinked with each other, and Competence is no different. Each of them are equal to each other, but for different reasons. Competence speaks directly to your skills as a Leader, and either you are competent as a Leader, or you're not. Don't worry though, as with all 12 C's, being competent as a Leader is something that can be learned.

Show me your followers and I will show you your future.

The key to your competency as Leader is empowering your Followers to do their best:

- **Delegate Power**

  Delegate power to your better Followers by making them Leaders of the group. We often call them Leads, who are given extra responsibility. Unlike Managers, they are even closer to other Followers, allowing them to have more rapport and direct encouragement that neither the Leader or Manager can do.

  Delegation of power has the obvious benefit of freeing space on your already full plate, but it gives your Followers something to shoot for within the group. While some are there to collect a paycheck and go home, others want to be in a Management or Leadership position, but those jobs are hard to come by and are often filled by people outside the company. A position created between Followers and Managers can often be a liaison position to get an ear of the Followers, but also a stepping stone for Followers to show their Leadership potential.

- **Make a Family**

  We are social creatures, and we want to feel a part of something, especially in a social sense. One good way is to encourage your Followers to not only to be a team but to be a family. Family is there for each other, they guide each other when they are behind, and pick each other up when they fall.

  How much you want to foster this is up to you, but if you can get your Followers to form a bond with each other, then they will become more productive and have an improved morale, especially if they feel their efforts are making a difference.

- **Cut the Fat**

  While this book tried to approach the positive aspects of Leadership, we also discuss the not so pretty elements. One element that is the most despised is firing. This makes use of Courage, to do what is necessary.

  If a Follower is not doing their best work, and in fact consistently under performs, then you need to let them go. There is only so much you can do to help someone be their best, and at the end of the day, they've got to want to be their best.

  This is a true test of your Competence as Leader. You should never fire as a way to inspire other workers, but it is not fair to keep someone on who is not towing the line.

  Other Followers work hard, and they deserve to be acknowledged for their work, but keeping on a bad Follower sends the message that either their Leader doesn't respect them, or they don't need to try as hard.

- **Help Settle Conflict**

  Conflict will happen amongst your Followers for a variety of reasons. Whether it is with other Followers or with themselves. Often, Followers want to go to the highest source they can to get resolution, and while you want to give them that resolution, you've got a lot to do as it is.

  The best way to deal with this is not to be their first stop. This makes use of delegation mentioned earlier, and in the case of conflict, you need to tell your Followers to solve things at the lowest level possible.

Having Team Leaders can often help direct Followers to the right resources to have Followers solve problems on their own. Failing that, it can go to the Managers who have more authority, and are used to help put out fires among the Followers, as discussed in *Leading And/Or Managing*. If the Manager is unable to resolve the conflict, then this should be brought to you. And of course, if you can't solve it, escalate it as necessary.

Teams should resolve their own problems and only come to you if the necessary steps fail. Followers may still try to skip steps, to which your response is to determine what their Team Leaders and Managers had to say on the issues; primarily if they were consulted or not, and if necessary, for the Followers to be directed to them or not.

- **Incentivize Performance**
  As Peter Gibbons demonstrated in the movie "Office Space", his only motivation was to not to lose his job. As businesses become more demanding, the more morale is affected.

  It's not like being on a farm and letting the work speak for itself... being in a business feels to many Followers as being another cog in the machine. I'm sure you can imagine that is not a great feeling.

  Some look at Incentivizing Performance as bribing people to work harder, but a bribe would indicate that you pay them first and then they do it. Using incentivization allows you to let the Followers know that there is a direct benefit to working hard beyond the completion of the goal, and you are rewarding the go-getters who are trying their hardest and meeting the demands.

This is not something to do all that often, as it will transform that their work is dependent on a prize to be won. At the same time, a once in a while gift for hard work can help stimulate work productivity. It's all about timing. This can also be of benefit for crucial stages of projects.

- **Set Milestones**
  The best way to deal with a project, especially a complex one, is to break it up into smaller pieces. Breaking into smaller pieces, also known as Milestones, help make a project seem more doable. It also has the added benefit to your Followers to have a sense of accomplishment for the project itself.

  A common approach to Milestones is to start with easier ones first, and eventually build up into hard tasks as you approach the end. This is a mistake to do. Followers will notice the pattern of it getting increasingly difficult, and upon completing a difficult Milestone, will feel defeated before the next Milestone even starts. This will affect productivity.

  A great workaround to this problem is to intermix the difficulty of Milestones. Start off easy and work your way up towards difficult, but offer short Milestones of easier tasks. Obviously, certain Milestones must be completed at certain times, and you cannot control their difficulty, but other ones you do have a level of control. If necessary, take a harder Milestone and break that up into easier tasks.

All of these are really just simple tasks that you should already be doing, but will allow you to maximize the productivity of your Followers, putting them at their best. Their best reflects well on you.

Remember that it is easy to look good with a team that is already amazing, but you rarely have an amazing team right from the beginning. More often, you will have a team of Followers who are lacking their best effort, and your competency as a Leader is what will guide them to their best.

In every field, there is one person who is the best. That person might not always be recognized as the best, and there can be some disagreement on the criteria used for any given subject, but objectively speaking, that person does exist.

If it is your passion and your goal is to be that person, then I wish you luck in what will be a monumental task. However, to be the best as a team, as a group, and as an organization, that's a much more realistic and attainable goal; merely find the best people you can, lead them well, and let them do what they do best.

Now, that's not to say that personal excellence is underrated; not at all. What it means is, if you are a running a pizzeria, you don't have to be the best pizza maker; you don't have to be the best delivery driver; you don't have to be the best server or accountant. It's okay if you are, but it's not necessary. What is necessary is that you know the best when you see it, can train them to be the best and can lead them to give you their best.

Personal growth and the continued pursuit of knowledge is a hallmark of great Leaders. Successful people never stop learning, and effective Leader never stop learning.

Reading is to the mind, what exercise is to the body.
-Joseph Addison

Effective Leaders share many traits, and one of these is often an appetite for books, whether paper or virtual. The Web is a tremendous boon to mankind, allowing one to read books online, on the computer screen, as an e-book, or sitting down with a dusty old volume and turning page after page.

While you will never learn all there is to learn, the is no limit to what you can learn when you make the effort to do so.

Presidents Thomas Jefferson, Abraham Lincoln, Theodore Roosevelt, and George Washington were all known not only as great Leaders but as obsessive readers. Jefferson built a rotating book stand so he could read five at once; Roosevelt, according to his biographer, would read 2-3 books on a free evening (only one book if it was a busy night); Washington had no formal education, but his personal library alone consisted of over 900 books.

While reading alone does not make someone an effective Leader, this is where the knowledge is stored. What you read matters - whether it is fiction, science, politics, biography, or another subject, it's important to be selective of what you should read in pursuit of being a better writer, though it's okay to read for enjoyment.

The more that you READ, the more things you will KNOW. The more that you LEARN, the more places you'll GO.
-Dr. Seuss

COMMON SENSE

The most powerful tool in your toolbox: don't leave it at home.

Why am I doing this report?
Why are we taking this path?
Why is this person in charge of that task?
Why? Why? Why?

We've discussed so far about the need for innovation. Businesses thrive when they innovate, and yet, there is still a strong desire to hold onto traditions.

Why?

Simply put, we as humans don't like change. Yet we know from past experiences of the last 30 years, that unless a company innovates, it dies.

This is the conundrum of Common Sense. We know what we should do, we have evidence to support it, and yet, we don't do it. We have established ways of doing things, and those ways make us money. Embracing innovation forces us to go into the unknown, uncertain of what the outcome will be. So why face the unknown?

Better the devil you know, than the devil you don't.

Unfortunately, it isn't so easy to think less of someone who is fearful of innovation. Innovation is the unknown, as it often means that no one has done it before, and it's uncertain if it will succeed or not, and if it does, to what degree.

It's not just your decision as a Leader alone, but as we state in *Compassion*, it is also that of your Followers and the business as a whole. If you're wrong, it could cost jobs and reputation of the company. It's something you must carefully balance when it comes to the decision of innovation.

This chapter however, speaks more to the ways of old in face of the modern age, and the adherence to traditions that fly in the face of Common Sense. You have to understand that the business world has changed in many different ways, from innovation in technologies to change of attitude in Followers. These changes came about for a variety of reasons, but whatever those were, this is now the standard, and most traditions of old no longer stand-up to what is needed today, so it makes little (Common) Sense to hold onto those traditions.

If you're going to be a Leader, you need to have the Common Sense to see that some traditions are past their prime, and you need to stop their use in order to cultivate an environment that is adaptable to the modern age. Business is no longer that of endurance, but that of change.

The following are things you can do to embrace the Common Sense of our modern era while dumping the traditions of old:

- **Long Term Solutions**

  Many companies have ran into problems because when faced with a difficult situation, they must make a decision between a short-term or a long-term resolution. The long-term has the potential to actually solve problems, but as the name suggests, takes a long time to implement. Short-term however, will very likely not resolve the overall issue, but fix something minor in a short amount of time.

  Traditionally, companies have picked the short-term solution, as that promised more immediate results, even if the problem itself remained. Companies would attempt a series of short-term solutions, generally hoping that the problem would either solve itself, or their series of short-term solutions would provide a long-term resolution.

  As a Leader of today, you must see that this flies in the face of Common Sense. If an action plan doesn't resolve an issue, then why do it? All it does is waste resources.

  This of course becomes a challenge as there may be some traditional Leaders who want immediate results, and a Leader can feel pressured to take on a short-term solution to make it seem like they are making a difference. A good way to deal with this is to take a long-term solution and break it up into a series of short-term solutions, or Milestones.

- **Adapt Projects**

  The traditional way of handling a project is to design how you will accomplish the task right from the beginning, and no matter what happens along the way, you must adhere to the initial plan.

125

The problem this presents is that new business solutions are coming out on an almost daily fashion. These new solutions should not only be embraced by companies but that their projects should change how they do things if there is a better way to do it.

The challenge with this is the cost and time implementation it takes and the deadline of the project. Common Sense would tell us that if the implementation takes longer than the deadline allows for, then we shouldn't do it. However, if the delay would be minor, then we listen to Common Sense and we do it.

Remember that in Courage, we state that we shouldn't be indifferent to consequences, and with innovation, we should do our homework on the benefits to any project we're on, to make sure it can actually improve the project itself.

Common Sense tells us that we shouldn't be so all-or-nothing with a project, and not be so quick to ignore innovation in favor of the tradition of completing something on how it was initially set to do, but not rush into innovation without doing our homework.

- **Reward Work**
  The old ways of doing things is to reward the potential someone has. Being of good pedigree, going to the right schools, and working in the right places; it was believed that if an individual was brought up in the right environment, they could do great things. Perhaps there is some truth to that, but all it really means is that those individuals are likely to be of the same ilk of the past.

In our modern world, the Common Sense thing to do is to reward workers who actually contribute, to reward for work done and not the potential someone might possess. Followers need to be as adaptive to the change that happens, and those who put in the extra effort should be recognized for that.

- **Create Value**
  While profit is necessary for a business to survive, it is no longer the only goal. Whether it is interaction with customers or building a product, what you and your Followers do must have value. We live in a world today where a bad comment on a website could cost a business a lot of money. Profit has to be balanced with doing something right.

Modernization over Traditions is really an issue of Common Sense. In this world today, a lot is talked about in the loss of tradition, cited as the main cause of the decline of America. If the loss of traditions were the decline of America and America has been in a decline for as long as people have claimed... it would no longer exist.

Remember that many traditions we have now was once a novel idea that replaced another tradition much older. It likely was met with a lot of resistance, and it took time for it to be a part of our world, to the point that people are not so willing to give it up.

We do speak a lot about modernization, about adapting to the new times, but it is important to remember that Common Sense is not against Traditions, but neither does it trust them. Common sense takes every tradition and subjects it to a thorough vetting process, an interrogation of the mind, with the ultimate goal of determining whether that tradition deserves to survive. We have always done it that way... is an obscenity... unless it is followed with a very, very good reason.

I am, as I've said, merely competent. But in an age of incompetence, that makes me extraordinary.

-Billy Joel

COLLABORATIVE SPIRIT

Harness the power of human capital, it will always serve you well.

Again, we are all in this together. When you consider what people can accomplish together that could never – literally never – be accomplished alone, one begins to wonder why so many Leaders attempt to go at it alone.

Think of what it took for the Apollo astronauts to land on the moon, the sheer number of people who were involved in that effort. From the astronauts themselves to the human computers who did the math, which made the science possible... it was an amazing achievement that only happened because of the Collaborative Spirit.

The sports metaphor is perhaps overused, but only because it is so applicable to these factors as well as so many others. The 1980 US Olympic hockey team had about a dozen players who played in the NHL after their Miracle on Ice, but most only played a short time and none could be considered superstars. On the other hand, the Soviet team was made up of many superstars who not only had successful careers in the USSR, but many went on to be top stars in the NHL.

On paper, there was no comparison; this was not a fair contest. Yet, when the game was over the USA team had won. Coach Herb Brooks had instructed in the team not only in hockey skills and play-making, but the concept that people who work together will always be stronger than those who work well but separately.

This does not mean teams cannot use stars. Stars are terrific! Think of Wayne Gretzky, to extend the sports analogy a little further. He was an amazing individual talent, who scored more goals than any other person in the history of the NHL.

What is lost on many people, though, is that Wayne Gretzky had more than twice as many assists than goals! Think about that – he helped others with their goals more than twice as often as he achieved them himself, and for that he is considered the greatest to play the game.

A quote from Herb Brooks stands out to me as we talk about the power of collaborative efforts. Coach brooks said to the 1980 Olympic hockey team during a practice:

"When you pull on that jersey, you represent yourself and your teammates. And the name on the front is a hell of a lot more 'important' than the one on the back! Get that through your head!"

Leaders of old have always stood on the shoulders of those who put in the work, taking the credit for something they couldn't do on their own. In the 12 C's, we speak a lot about teamwork and collaboration, but the most important aspect to know: As Leader, you are not the star of the show. You are but a member of the team, just as Herb Brooks was not their coach, but also a member of the team with a role to play.

If there is a star of your team, it is Collaborative Spirit, the collective of people that make up your Followers, and us as Leaders being a part of them to become more than the sum of our individual parts.

Unlike the other 12 C's, this doesn't have a small list of things to consider or do to accomplish the 12 C's. Collaborative Spirit is just a mindset, and you are stronger with your team than doing it alone, and it is a mentality you must maintain. However, it is still a skill and requires you to actively engage in it to build up your skill.

Leaders do not seek personal individual accolades. They may come, naturally, but that is not the goal. What the group accomplishes is all that matters.

I'm pretty good with collaborative thinking. I work well with other people.

-David Bowie

COMMUNICATOR

**Communicate with everyone, even
your adversaries.**

Like Collaborative Spirit, this one is talked a lot about throughout this book, though for this one, it is discussed in detail in: *Is Communication an Automatic Transfer?* While that chapter goes into great lengths of how to communicate effectively, and some of the pitfalls of bad communication, there is a difference in knowing how to communicate, and the frequency in which you do it. Remember: the ideas which are not shared, and the messages not sent, are worthless. We outlined the communication process, and it is worth looking again at the Transactional Model for Communication:

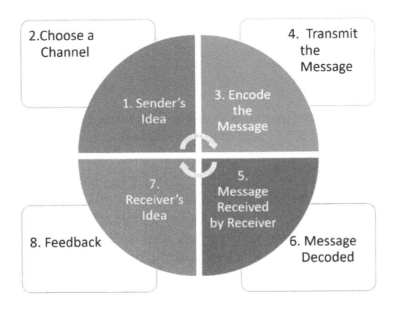

I won't go over these 8 steps again, as there is a chapter that already does that. I will however go into the importance of communicating often.

Many Leaders try to spend as little time with their Followers as possible, and this often creates an added level of intimidation. Your Followers shouldn't fear you as the boss automatically. They should respect you and understand the authority you have.

Many Leaders of the past favor the writings of Machiavelli, in the concept of whether it is better to be loved or feared. Machiavelli wrote that it is better to have both, to be loved and feared, but being both is quite difficult, and if you have to choose one, you should choose fear, as those in fear of you are less likely to act against you.

Many have tried to apply Machiavellian practices in the workplace, and I argue against this. Your goal should never be to be feared, as workers today know they can find somewhere else to work. Employment is a free market, and if they don't work for you, then they move on.

Now I'm not saying your goal should be to be loved, as that doesn't help you either. The key aspect is to be respected, and for you to show that respect back. Respect is earned, it is never granted.

I know it seems like I've gotten off on a tangent here, but I promise you that this does tie into being an effective Communicator. To be respected as a Leader, your Followers know that you are someone they can rely on, someone who will lead them. Followers put their faith in you, and as their Leader, you need to deliver them to the promised land (metaphorically speaking, of course).

It's a tall order to fill... so how do you deliver? There isn't any one thing you can do, or rather, there are multiple ways you can do that, including those featured in the 12 C's, but communication is a cardinal option for how to effectively lead. Consider the alternative, to lead by not communicating at all, or very little. How effective do you think you'll be?

This goes back to being Intentional and The Law of Attraction, that the attitude you set should be Intentional, in the manner of influencing your Followers. You would want them to come to you if there is a concern, you want them to give to the company that gives to them. So why is it necessary for them to communicate, but less important for a Leader? In truth, it is not.

Having face time with the boss is beneficial, as it can improve morale and Followers can humanize with their Leader. Humanizing their Leader means they will want to work harder for their Leader.

However, face time is not always possible, and an email can still go a long way, but try to avoid a cookie-cutter email that was just put together on the fly and has little thought to it. Your Followers are not stupid, and they can see when their boss is giving less than their best, and they will likely take it personally.

Just like Collaborative Spirit, there isn't a list of things for you to do or consider. This comes down to practice. Look over the Transactional Model for Communication in the last chapter of Part I to understand how communication works, and how to diagnose any problems that may occur when it comes to giving a message, idea, or vision.

Like all the other 12 C's, being a Communicator is a learned skill, and like all learned skills, it requires practice. Practice, simply put, means doing it with intention. It is impossible to become adept at a skill by merely reading about it, thinking about it, pondering it. We often admire a man of few words, but rarely can that apply to a Leader, because a Leader must share with their Followers, and often!

To be a good Comunicator, you must make sure that at any given time, your Followers understand where they are and where they are going. Followers can never be allowed to be lost when working towards a project, and any instance they are, it is the Leader who must communicate to them what they need to be doing.

However, there is a fine balance between just enough and too much communication. How you determine that is up to you and your unique situation, but a good rule of thumb, is just enough that keeps your Followers productive. If they are not productive, then communication is required.

Speech is power: Speech is to persuade, to convert, to compel.
-Emerson

CONVICTION

**Like a dog with a bone, you must
know what you desire the most.**

Understand that what you desire may not be what you artic-
ulate, or even what you really want. Many people believe that
what they want is the next rung on the ladder, the next title,
the next level of power. I did. I spent my entire career thinking that what I wanted was that next title and the pay that
went along with it.

I got to the top, I became the CEO of a company, and when I
realized that there was nowhere else for me to go, I was still
unfulfilled. That's when the truth came to me. It wasn't the
title or the pay or the power or the parking spot that I
wanted; I wanted to influence people in a positive manner.

I became a motivational speaker and author, because that all
along was what I really wanted, even though for the longest
time I didn't realize that true fulfillment for me was to enable
the success of others.

It can be difficult to find what you desire the most. It can involve so many factors, including money, family, personal goals, society as a whole, and more. This is an exercise in selfishness, because until you have become – for the moment – completely selfish, you will not be able to see what you want in your heart of hearts.

> ***Many men go fishing all of their lives without knowing that it is not fish they are after.***
> -Henry David Thoreau

We must find the conviction to seek the truth. I have been asked many times over this simple question. "If you were to win the lottery today, what would you "choose" to do tomorrow?" My answer has always been that I would go back to work, not because I want more money but because in my life I need to be surrounded by people that want more.

Apathy can only be overcome by enthusiasm. I crave enthusiasm and abhor apathy. To find your passion and your enthusiasm, you must find what brings you joy and what brings you bliss. Once you find joy, you will become that "dog with a bone", the man deserted on an island that simply wants a drink of water. Find this simple "true north" and you will pursue it with the fervor of conviction.

> ***The final test of a Leader is that he leaves behind him in other men the conviction and the will to carry on.***
> -Walter Lippmann

Do you have conviction in your life right now, is the role in your career a source of passion for you? Honestly, being Leader on a day-to-day basis can be scary. There is a lot of uncertainty, there is a lot of decisions we must make, and rarely do we truly understand the consequences of those decisions.

It's OK to have fear, so long as you don't let it overwhelm you. Even with passion, there is room for fear, as fear keeps you hyper-aware and on your toes, and prevents mistakes.

To be a Leader, you must handle uncertainty, and you must handle it so your Followers know that things are good and they can carry on their day. This is where conviction comes into play, this is where passion comes in, as passion and conviction can carry us on when fear threatens to take over.

Consider the movie, "_A Few Good Men_". Throughout the movie, Lt. Daniel Kaffee shows his conviction for his job as a lawyer, even to the point of arguing with another lawyer (while practicing at a baseball diamond), refusing the offer he is being given and pushing the other lawyer into what he wants. The other lawyer asks, "I don't know why I'm agreeing to this?" Obviously, the other lawyer has no conviction in what he does, no drive or passion, unlike Lt. Kaffee.

Taking another example from that move, at the end, when it was the passion and conviction of Lt. Kaffee when he had Col. Nathan Jessep on that stand, and he was attempting to ask a question that could end his career... if he ordered the code red, basically an accusation that Jessep did something he knew he shouldn't have done. If you watch that movie again, watch Kaffee drink the water, he is shaking.

As we discussed in Courage, being brave is not the lack of fear, but the ability to act in spite of the fear. It is the same with Conviction, that it is not the lack of fear, but that your Conviction can carry you on in the face of fear.

When you have Conviction, you have strength, you have Character, you have Courage. Though it may not seem like it, showing Conviction is a skill, and it does take practice. If you can master showing Conviction, then you will succeed in The Law of Attraction and Transactional Model of Communication. Below are some things you can do.

- **Don't Be Harsh**
  Some Leaders in their attempt to show their Conviction, end up becoming a Drill Sargent, using their shouting voices to get their Followers to carry out their passion. You may feel that your passion fills you with energy, and the excitement you have needs to be shouted, but that shouting will often be seen as you being a tyrant. When you share your passion, use your gentle side to show it.

> *Thaw with her gentle persuasion is more powerful than Thor with his hammer. The one melts, the other breaks into pieces.*
> -Henry David Thoreau

- **Share Your Passion**
  This goes with Communicator, that when you have such Conviction of your vision, of what it is that you're wanting to do, it is important that your Followers know about it. Be Intentional, and show how you feel, and encourage your Followers to have the same passion as you, let them see the passion you have. The Law of Attraction is a very real thing, and if they understand why you feel as you do, then they are likely to emulate it themselves, or even develop that passion.

- **Don't Be Cocky**
  With passion and Conviction, you feel a great sense of pride. You know that what you're doing is right, and it is easy to let that carry you away. Leaders especially can become cocky, as very few can tell them that they are overdoing their passion.

  It's good to think you're right, but remember to have humility in the process, to remember that just because you have strong Convictions, doesn't mean you are infallible, and still need to listen to the voices of your Followers, especially if they disagree with you. In their disagreement, you may find something you overlooked and can improve your plan or vision.

- **Live It, Not Preach It**
  Another instance of being Intentional, that when you have passion, to show you have Passion. It is one thing to share it, to let people know you have it and encourage them to have it, but it's another thing to constantly talk about it and push others to have it the same, and show little contempt for those who don't share it. After all, it is your passion; it is your Conviction and no one else's. If you want others to embrace it, live your Conviction and let others see that you have it.

If you lack Conviction, if you cannot find passion in what you're doing, then it might be time to move on from where you are. A Leader without Conviction is just a person with a fancy title awaiting their next promotion. Don't be that person. If this is the job you want, then have the Conviction to keep it, and share that with your Followers.

> *Without conviction, nothing really matters, and nothing of significance is passed on.*
> -R. Albert Mohler Jr.

CAPACITY

Internalize your problems, until it turns into a vision.

This is perhaps the most difficult of our "C's" to instruct on, as it involved a change of perspective that many people have been trained not to accept. We must have the Capacity to internalize our problems until they turn into visions.

You've heard it offered as a cliché that there are no problems, only opportunities. Well, that maxim is crap. There are real problems, and it is foolish to pretend they don't exist; but problems short of death can be overcome.

Another maxim that is crap is "living without regret". You hear this a lot, that you shouldn't live without regrets. The basic idea is that you live your life to the fullest, and not live with the regret that you didn't do something when you had the opportunity. The problem is that our mistakes are crucial to us as individuals.

The risk of a wrong decision is preferable to the terror of indecision.

-Maimonides

What happens to us is that we spend so much time worrying about the problem, seeing the terrible impact it will bring to us, that we forget to concentrate on the solution. More than that, we use our problems as limitations, and we begin to see life as a series of limitations, and dare I say, we become addicted to limitations... the more we have, the more we feel at ease.

That last part sounds strange, but as the saying goes, "Misery loves company", and when we feel bad or feel unable to do something, in a sense, we feel better. Don't get me wrong, we still feel bad we can't do something we know we need to, but there is a sense of relief that if we can't do something, then we shouldn't try.

The lesson is not to ignore your troubles, not to ignore the problems in your life or business. Many "self-help gurus" will tell you to ignore the bad and focus on the good, but in reality, success does not come from affirmations and useless mantras. Ignoring the negative and only focus on the positive is the kind of thinking as Leaders that we need to snap out of.

Just because an obstacle is before us in our path, doesn't mean we should give up at the first opportunity, or even pretend that there is no obstacle and walk in a different direction.

The way you deal with an obstacle is to deal with the obstacle. Some obstacles must be climbed over; some obstacles must be crashed through; some obstacles must be walked around. When none of these work, the Leader considers more, and never gives up; they dig under the obstacle... they find a helicopter and flies over the top... they negotiate with the wall and asks it to move.

> *The successful Leader has the capacity to be patient and persistent at the same time. The successful Leader never gives up, because as long as there is breath, there is hope.*

Humans are amazingly adept at self-fulfilling prophesies. Our ability to accomplish most tasks is directly correlated to our belief that we can do it. It's important to note here that this does not mean that belief alone will get the task done, and it would be foolish to believe that. Capacity alone will accomplish very little, you still need intelligence, education, skills, and the other of the 12 C's.

Dorothea Brande is not a name well known today, but in the 1930s she wrote, *Wake Up and Live,* a book on success which sold millions of copies. Her formula for success has an element which speaks to the human Capacity, and I would like to borrow it here. Once we have determined what our solutions might be, there is something to "break the spell of inertia and frustration" which accompanies all difficult tasks: Act as if it were impossible to fail.

Consider this: While failure is always possible, there is nothing to be gained, and much to lose, by letting our minds think about those consequences. There is everything to be gained by reason-based confidence.

The actions should be the same no matter what our attitude, but we know the power of humanity for self-fulfilling prophesies, so Brande's advice is perfect: for as long as you are working on the solution to your problem, act as if it were impossible to fail, and your efforts will be the best they can. Your capacity to endure will strengthen.

> *Do what you love; gnaw your*
> *own bone; gnaw at it, bury it,*
> *unearth it, and gnaw at it still.*
> -Henry David Thoreau

Having Capacity means to have the ability or power to do something, to have the experience, or even have the understanding of something. Leaders need to have the Capacity to look at their problems, but not as limitations, but for what they truly are, obstacles to overcome.

To have Capacity is also an element of the Law of Attraction. The Law of Attraction is not about having the right outward attitude, as many believe it is... the Law of Attraction is about moving all elements of you forward.

The Law of Attraction requires some darker colors on the canvas, so the brighter ones look more radiant. In ignoring your problems, you might well seem like a positive individual, but it means that you are setting yourself up for failure.

By ignoring your problems, you are not properly using failure, and when you don't learn from your failure, you are doomed to repeat your failures. While you try to remain positive for the sake of the Law of Attraction, in turn, you are passing off your fear of your problems, which will have a greater blowback than actually acknowledging your problems and dealing with them.

Don't ignore your problems, don't avoid obstacles. Deal with them. More importantly, have the Capacity to believe you can overcome them, have the Capacity to believe that there is a solution, and have the Capacity to do what needs to be done.

Now you can see why Capacity is so important to be a Leader, because without it, so much else falls short. Without Capacity, we simply give up. Without Capacity, we focus on the problem to the detriment of the solution. Without Capacity, we don't learn from our mistakes, our regrets, and continually make the same errors that we have before. Instead, we must find a solution for obstacles by having the Capacity to believe we can overcome.

The greater the problem,
the greater is our need for
the capacity to see beyond
them, and find a solution.

Or, as Captain Taggert from the film Galaxy Quest would say, "Never give up – Never surrender!"

Leadership is the capacity to
translate vision into reality.
-Warren Bennis

CREDIBILITY

Integrity is expressed in what you do, not in what you say.

By the time you have read this book, most of you already have an image of the type of Leader you are or will be. Whether you call it brand, reputation, or something else, it is what people think of when they think of you. It might not be the brand you want because so much of our brand is created unintentionally when we don't make a conscious effort to create it intentionally.

This is where Credibility comes in. We must be Intentional in our actions, but there has to be a level of integrity behind it. Not just some integrity, but everything you do has to be with Integrity First, as mentioned in Character. Only with being Intentional and using integrity behind your actions, can you then have Credibility.

When it comes to having Credibility, it is all about decisions you make. To borrow from Robert Redford and the film, "*Lions For Lambs*", that even before you are given that fancy title and that parking space, before you give your first command, your Credibility as Leader is measured.

You being Leader started before you were officially a Leader based on many of the decisions you've made as Leader, and by the time you were recognized as a Leader, you were already a dozen decisions into the role.

Because you had already made decisions into the role of Leadership before you were a Leader, that has an effect on your Credibility. Many believe that a promotion comes with a clean slate, a new beginning. A promotion doesn't come with those things, and the Credibility you have before carries over. Just because your Followers might be too scared to voice their opinions, doesn't mean that they see you in a positive light, especially if you were once their peer.

Even with the decisions you had when you came into the role as Leader, or any past decision you've had as Leader up to this date, those of which have created your brand as Leader and had an impact on your Credibility, still affect you.

The good news is that your brand can begin to change. Your brand can change today, if that is your intention. In fact, it will whether you intend it to or not, but as we have seen, intention more likely leads to positive results than do accidents, thanks to the Law of Attraction. Every single day, in tiny steps and small doses, you impact your brand.

Five years from now you will be a different person than you are today. Ten years from now you'll be a different person still. We all have things we regret from earlier in our lives, and we will all regret decisions from this year somewhere down the road.

We change, constantly, but change in consistency to the decisions and mistakes we make. We may not always see the change in ourselves, but if you run into someone you haven't seen in many years, chances are you'll be struck by just how much that person has changed over the years. Politically, socially, personally; we are in a constant state of change.

Your brand changes with every decision you make, or the current brand is strengthened by that decision, so make sure that what you do is Intentional, and make sure that you are not merely giving lip service to that brand. Your Followers will not be fooled. It is another cliché to say that actions speak louder than words, but it is wrong only because it doesn't go far enough:

Actions speak;
Words, by comparison, are silent.

Leadership is not decreed by position; it is decided and decreed by the Followers, individually and collectively, and it will be based on your integrity, not your title. The Leader is not necessarily the boss, and the boss may not be a Leader. When they are combined in the same person the level of influence is increased, but Leaders come from everywhere in an organization, from everywhere within a team.

Some Leaders are born, but many Leaders simply dared to ask the question why and rose to a position of powers by help from their Followers. They built their Credibility, by showing integrity with each decision they made. They made mistakes, as we all do, but they didn't hide from them, they didn't deny themselves the lessons to be learned by them, and over time, became the hero we remember them as.

It is a myth that Leaders are all-powerful and all-important in the traditional sense. It's a myth that a good, strong Leader is infallible and incapable of making mistakes. Leaders need their Followers just as much as Followers need their Leaders. In this way, Leaders exist at every level and for every purpose. Leaders influence people's lives; that makes someone a Leader, whether they are already a Leader, or become a new Leader.

As the final C in our list, it comes down to Credibility. All of them are important, all of them are necessary for you to be a Leader, but none of it means anything without the Credibility of your Leadership. You could have the other 11 but lack Credibility, and still be a poor Leader because you don't have your Follower's trust.

> ### *To be persuasive we must be believable; to be believable we must be credible; to be credible we must be truthful.*
> -Edward R. Murrow

With that said, if you are a new Leader, or an established Leader needing to rebuild your Credibility, there are things you can do. Understand, as mentioned in the Laws of Attraction, as Leader, you are under a microscope, and your Followers are waiting for you to fail. One mistake can outshine any accomplishment you made prior, and depending on the severity, accomplishments made after.

Rebuilding Credibility is no easy feat, and there is nothing I can tell you here that will make it a quick fix for you. Below are some suggestions, by no means will guarantee success. The only way you can succeed is if there is integrity behind what you do from now on.

- **Give Trust**

  To have trust, you must give trust. How can Followers trust you if you don't trust them? Starting in a disadvantaged position, you will need to give more trust at first than you will receive, but over time that power dynamic will shift into a more equitable balance of a more give and take dynamic.

- **Show Transparency**

  You can't reveal everything about what you do with your Followers, as that is the nature of business. However, there are things you can tell them, and you should tell them.

  When there is transparency, your Followers can see that you are working in their interests, even if you must make a decision that works against their interests. It's when they are left in the dark about something; they let their distrust turn to paranoia. You can't control how they react, but if you show them transparency when you can, then it is easier for them to trust you when you can't.

- **Practice the 12 C's**

  When there is a loss of respect, improving any of the 12 C's can help you through gaining respect, and can especially help you establish Credibility. The 12 C's are all interconnected together, and as you improve one, the others will flourish. I will recommend not to do one at a time, or not to focus on just one for very long without doing another on the 12 C's.

- **Delegate Responsibilities**

  It can be difficult to regain the Credibility of a whole group. Alternatively, you can usually win the trust of an individual faster, and have them help you build your credibility.

Promoting a Lead who can act as a liaison can help them help the others to put their trust in you. This can be a great benefit to you, so it is important that you don't misuse this trust by manipulating your Lead. They are a tool for you to be an effective Leader, but they are also a person, a human being, and unlike an inanimate tool, this one can react badly if misused. Treat this very seriously, and utilize the tips to build Credibility.

Having Credibility is tantamount to having your Follower's respect. Remember that. Some may try to use Credibility as a popularity contest, that they believe that the trust they have means they are well liked, or try to become well-liked believing it gives them Credibility as a Leader.

As a Leader, your job is not to be liked, it is to be Respected. Of course, you can be respected and be liked, which is often far better than to be Respected and feared... but between being liked and being respected, respect is your #1 goal.

> *You can't lead the people if*
> *you don't love the people.*
> *You can't save the people if*
> *you don't serve the people.*
> -Cornel West

PART III – PUTTING THE PIECES TOGETHER

If you've made it this far, and have read this in order, then by this point, you have read what the image of a Leader should be and what those pieces of the puzzle are to make that image. Now, it's all about putting together the puzzle. It starts with the right attitude, and then you can begin to assemble the sections of the puzzle together to create the picture of the leader that you will be.

THE ATTITUDE OF A LEADER

By now, you should have reviewed the 12 C's, and hopefully you have thought about where you are personally in the spectrum as it relates to the C's. What I can assure you is that whether you think you are doing well or whether you think there are areas for improvement, what I know is that we all can be more thoughtful and more intentional with everything we do. It all starts with having the right attitude.

The attitude of a Leader can make or break them. We sometimes hear about attitude as a bad thing, or a cocky thing, or something that gets in our way. Someone shared with me almost 20 years ago this quote from Charles Swindoll and it has been something that I have come back to repeatedly in my life. Please pause for just a moment, take a deep breath and then read this quote on the next page with focus and intent on understanding.

The longer I live, the more I realize the impact of attitude on life. Attitude, to me, is more important than facts. It is more important than the past, than education, than money, than circumstances, than failures, than successes, than what other people think or say or do. It is more important than appearance, giftedness, or skill. It will make or break a company... a church... a home.

The remarkable thing is we have a choice every day regarding the attitude we will embrace for that day. We cannot change the inevitable. The only thing we can do is play on the one string we have, and that is our attitude...

I am convinced that life is 10% what happens to me, and 90% how I react to it. And so it is with you... we are in charge of our Attitudes.

-Charles Swindoll

This quote will have different meanings to you at different times in your life. I know that for me, every time that I read it, I find a new thought or a new epiphany as it relates to where I am in my life at that moment.

A few weeks ago (at the time of this writing) I had yet another amazing life experience, and that was the opportunity to get married to an amazing woman. I would like to take a minute to tell you a story about this adventure that I believe fully illustrates the point that I am trying to make about attitude.

To set the stage, my wife is a very adventurous soul, and together we have a very large group of friends and family. We decided to get married in Merida, Mexico and we were able to have over 100 of our closest friends join us there. Two days before the wedding we had planned a couple of excursions for our family and friends to visit Chichen Itza with almost 40 people, and on the next day we took a group of almost 50 people to visit three amazing cenotes deep in the country of the Yucatan Peninsula.

If you're not familiar with cenotes, they are a natural occurrence of a sinkhole, resulting from the collapse of limestone bedrock that exposes beautiful fresh sweet water underneath. I encourage you to visit and swim in one someday if you have not had the fortune to do that in your life add it to your bucket list.

Now to the story, a dear friend of mine and her husband joined us on the trip and went on the adventures. The day that we went to the cenotes, we had rented a couple of large vans to transport everyone and drove for about 2 hours to a remote area where there were some rail carts pulled by horses that we had to take for about an hour deeper into the remote areas where the cenotes were.

Before we got on the carts there was a small building with some rudimentary bathrooms, that had toilets with no seats and no toilet paper. This is rather common in these areas of Mexico. One of my friends went to the bathroom, and she had explosive diarrhea. Imagine that, with no toilet paper and no seat. Wait, don't imagine that, it's not a good image to have. We heard her desperate cries through the building with no windows to see if anyone had any tissues. We were able to scrounge up what she needed.

I had learned later, during her time in the bathroom, she was stung by some sort of bug, which had a very adverse effect, causing a welt that went from the middle of her back to half-way down her leg.

In the midst of all of this, it was mid-morning and it was about 95 degrees with 90% humidity. To say the least, she was miserable and thinking now I have to get on this bumpy cart and ride for the next hour with this welt. Not being the type of person to hold up the group, she soldiered on and boarded the carts.

Now the cart ride was beautiful, though the biting flies and the stench of the horses was not pleasant, but it was part of the experience.

When we arrived at the first stop, we walked several hundred feet into the woods to discover this small hole in the ground of which we descended these rudimentary steps to see one of the most amazing sites of my life. About 75 feet down below this small hole was a pool of brilliant blue clear water in this cavernous hole. We all went down to swim in the cenote.

It was nothing short of amazing. We went on for the next few hours with continued bumpy cart rides, biting flies and seeing another amazing cenote.

At the end, we took the long cart ride back to the van, had some street food and the long ride back to town. When we got back to the beautiful house that we had rented on AirBNB, we poured a cocktail and were chatting.

This is when my friend recanted the stories that I did not know: all the details of the explosive diarrhea, the bug bite, etc. As she was telling us this story she told it with amazing and graphic detail and then she followed this horrific story with one statement that encapsulates attitude that I found perfect as part of the end of this book. She tells the story as any great storyteller would but then simply adds this sentence:

"And I would do it all again tomorrow if given half the chance."

This statement really illustrated to me that attitude can turn any negative situation into the right situation if you look at it the right way. As Leaders, we must adopt the attitude that the challenges that we face, the obstacle we encounter, the devastating blows are all part of the entire experience, they only become the experience if we quit because of those things.

Life is filled with some amazing experiences, but sometimes we don't get to the amazing end of the story because we let the little things that happen, paralyze us with fear and we give up. As a Leader, don't give up, you must soldier on, you must see the amazing things that are waiting for you at the end of the bumpy cart ride... and let the diarrhea and bug bites be damned.

To quote Charles Swindoll again:

"And so, it is with you... We are in charge of our attitudes"

YOU HAVE THE RIGHT PIECES NOW FINISH THE PUZZLE

This chapter is more of, "How to Use This Book", which traditionally is found at the front of books such as these. However, putting at the front of this book doesn't make sense, as you need to understand the nature of the puzzle before you can solve it.

In this book, we allude to a puzzle, or more specifically a jigsaw puzzle, to demonstrate that to be a Leader, or improve as a Leader, you need to think of the 12 C's as pieces in that puzzle and the idea of the Leader you want to be as the image to that jigsaw puzzle.

Think about that for a moment, what if you had all the pieces to a puzzle, say 10,000 pieces, but didn't know what the image was supposed to be... would you want to put that puzzle together? Likely no. If you're going to put this puzzle together, you need some sort of guideline to what the final image should be.

This book is very much like that. We could just go over the individual pieces, and make this book like 60 pages long. However, without understanding how to construct that image of what an ideal Leader is, then the 12 C's are not unlike that 10,000 jigsaw puzzle that you must build without knowing what the final image is.

You'll no doubt notice that the 12 C's are not only interconnected together, but interconnected with the image you build up of the ideal Leader you want to be. This is no accident, this is Intentional.

This book starts and stops with the same lesson: Be Intentional. When it comes to putting the puzzle together, it must be an intentional act. You must want to do this, and in order to be a good Leader, you must build the image, understand the pieces, and then put it all together.

The first step to being your ideal Leader is to build that image of what is the best Leader for you. You can't be Abraham Lincoln or even Martin Luther King Jr., as there were already was an Abraham Lincoln and Martin Luther King Jr. You can idolize them and appreciate those attributes that made them great, and even find inspiration from their example in developing yourself as a Leader... but your ideal image of a great Leader is the best Leader you can be.

Be yourself, everyone else is already taken.
-Cornel West

To start, we need to borrow a page from *Attributes of The Best and Worst Leaders* chapter. Take a step back and close your eyes, and think about yourself in two ways:

1. Think about who you are right now. Really think. Don't just focus on the good attributes you like about yourself, or the positive things people say about you, but dig deep inside and ask yourself some hard questions about who you are and where you are in life, and most importantly, where are you going. Ask the Who, What, Where, and Why of you right now.

2. Who do you ideally want to be, who is the Leader that you envision yourself to be. When you close your eyes, picture your office, picture the door closed, picture someone in that office.

Now walk into that office, and picture who is that person sitting in the chair, all dressed up, working hard on the day's work. Imagine someone comes in to ask something, imagine how that individual responds to that person, imagine their demeanor and posture, and then ask who they are, who they really are, ask them what they want, where they are going, and why are they this person.

So close your eyes, and think of those two people. Compare and contrast. Then imagine those two people going out to lunch and discussing your future. Imagine that idealized Leader, the future version of yourself, giving you advice on what you need to do next, imagine that person telling you ideas and suggestions found in this book. That person knows who you are, that person knows your strengths and weaknesses, and when they tell you what you need to do to become who they are, I want you to listen carefully.

Go ahead and close your eyes, and once they are done talking, I want you to write down what they've said. I'll wait.

...

...

...

I hope that was a rewarding experience. It will be different for everyone, but I will say that some of you might feel a bit down that you are not that person yet. Don't feel down, feel inspired that you could be that person, so long as you follow the advice they gave, advice you know because you read this book from cover to cover, and if you need to read it again, do so as many times as you need to.

With the image of who you want to be, and understand who you are, you should be able to pinpoint the things you need to do to accomplish that goal. Having read this book once already, your idealized self should be able to give you advice, and you should heed that advice. Write down what you need to do. Then write down the 12 C's:

- Courage
- Charisma
- Character
- Compassion
- Creativity
- Competence
- Common Sense
- Collaborative Spirit
- Communicator
- Conviction
- Capacity
- Credibility

With those twelve written down, I want you to circle the ones you think you are strong in, and then underline the ones you think you need to work on. Remember that it is very easy to lie to ourselves and for us to think we are good in all twelve. As confident as I am on these, and in the years I spent developing myself, I know that if I did this now, I very well would still underline a few of them. Not because I have failed in any way, but that as I develop myself as a Leader, I continually need to work on all of these.

So long as you remain a Leader, your development to become a good Leader never ends.

With those 12 C's circled and underline, you now need to construct the pieces. Remember who your idealized self is, and the great Leader they are. With that in mind, I want you to go through each of the ones you underline, and review each of them in this book.

I want you to write down each of the C's that are underlined, and write them on their own separate page. On each page, I want you to write down how you feel you are weak in that, and what steps you should do in order to build up your skill in that.

For example, let's pick Charisma. So, I would write Charisma at the top of a new piece of paper. Don't worry if you too picked Charisma, it's a common one chosen. I would then write how I might be weak in Charisma. Perhaps I write down a lack of confidence, or that I stutter, perhaps even I lack passion.

(You get the idea)

After I write down all of this, I look at it all together, all the pages and I start a new page, writing down what I must do to overcome those challenges that I have, how to improve on my skills. Given how interconnected all of this is, perhaps improving a fault actually improves several of the skills featured in this book.

For example, let's use a stuttering problem. Improving that would improve my Courage, Charisma, Characters, and even being a skilled Communicator.

Seems good so far, but we're not done yet. Now we focus on the ones we circled, and for each one of those, we write down what about them are we good at. Perhaps for Conviction, I write down that I really love what I do. I'm sure you're asking, is this really necessary? You feel that you are good at it, why spend time focusing on it at all?

Two reasons:

1. You will find that as you attempt to resolve the failings you have as a Leader, that it is your strength that will help you.

   In the example of stuttering being an issue, my Conviction will likely will be what will help me overcome my stuttering. By focusing on why I am passionate about my being a Leader, and keeping that in mind as I practice my speech, I'm quite certain it will help me overcome my stuttering problem.

2. Is it enough? I really love what I do, and that is great for Conviction, but is there anything more I can do?

   Writing this down and reading the chapter, I realize that I need to show it to others how important it is to me, let my Followers see my conviction and be inspired by it. Having written it down, I realize there is more I can do, that I might have otherwise overlooked.

So now you know what your weaknesses are, you know what your strengths are, you've determined that there are things you need to do to become a more effective Leader, and additionally, other things you can do to become even greater. That right there is how you use this book.

This book is your manual, and I recommend reading it two to three times a year, doing this exercise every time you do. Funny thing in our lives, what was once a weakness can become a strength, and what was once a strength can become a weakness without us ever realizing it. Reading this book might well help you discover that about yourself, so long as you remain truthful to yourself.

Leadership is an ongoing journey; one of which there is no stopping – unless you retire. Every day is a new challenge, every day you must make decisions, and every day you will be asked to juggle the world around you. No easy feat. I know, I am a Leader myself, and there really is no formal training on how to be a good Leader, and unfortunately it is a lot of trial and error.

I made this book with that in mind, to help you avoid some pitfalls along the way, especially in this newly evolving world where nothing is certain. This doesn't have answers for you, and there is no grand secret. To be your best, you must work to be your best.

This book is simply a road map on your journey, a guide to help you along the way, and one you should look at many times, especially when you get lost from your main path.

DECODING THE PUZZLE

Courage – Take a position even when it is painful.

Charisma – You must leverage your "influence" to get the job done.

Character – It's not written in your DNA but is who you are at the core; it is your "default position". Know yourself: Assess Evaluate and Correct.

Compassion – The most profound human emotion, a desire to alleviate another's suffering.

Creativity – Leaders "live" outside the box. Embrace change like it is your own child.

Competence – Surround yourself with the best, and you will be the best. Read voraciously.

Common Sense – The most powerful tool in your toolbox, don't leave it at home.

Collaborative Spirit – Harness the power of human capital, it will always serve you well.

Communicator – Communicate with everyone even your adversaries.

Conviction – Commitment -Like a dog with a bone, you must know what you desire the most.

Capacity – Internalize your problem until it turns into vision.

Credibility – Integrity is expressed in what you do, not what you say.

The Twelve C's of an Exceptional Leader

By: Richard George, NOI Coach

As a former property manager, the habits I learned and processes to which I became addicted have enabled me to thrive. I am addicted to reading, I am addicted to pursuing knowledge and I am addicted to making difficult situations simple. Leadership can be difficult and I continue to strive for its simplicity. Throughout my years of Leadership, I have diligently tried to isolate the characteristics of good Leaders. Many business books and ideological philosophies gave great insight to my quest, yet the real test was practicality and simple implementation.

I created my C-list of the Leadership characteristics to which I have become addicted. Each of these characteristics are derived and learned from my property management experiences and each is both practical and simple.

Rich George is the owner and managing director of NOI Coach, a business coaching, consulting and training firm based in Michigan. Known for his team building, culture changing, and change management skills, Rich's "no-nonsense" approach to problem solving has helped many people and companies accomplish their goals. www.NOIcoach.com